CATCHING GLIMPSES

CONSULTANTS

Mildred Bailey	**Teresa Flores**	**Nancy Mayeda**
Rose Barragan	**Charles Hacker**	**Kenneth Smith**
Barbara Burke	**P.J. Hutchins**	**Lydia Stack**
Barbara B. Cramer	**George Jurata**	**Mary Wigner**
Wilma J. Farmer		

Executive Editor: *Sandra Maccarone*

Senior Editor: *Ronne Kaufman*

Assistant Editor: *Suzanne M. Heller*

Design Director: *Leslie Bauman*

Assistant Design Director: *Kay Wanous*

Production Director: *Barbara Arkin*

Production Manager: *Trudy Pisciotti*

Cover, Front Matter, Unit Openers designed by: *Thomas Vroman Associates, Inc.* Illustrators: Tien Ho, pp. 14-23; Allen Davis, pp. 24-33; Angela Fernan, pp. 34-37; Lyle Miller, pp. 38-47; Allen Eitzen, pp. 48-52; Melanie Arwin, p. 53; Freya Tanz, pp. 56-67; Barbara McClintock, pp. 68-77; True Kelley, pp. 80-83; Gwen Brodkin, pp. 84-93; Karen Pellaton, pp. 94-102; Tien Ho, p. 103; Ethel Gold, pp. 106-115; Lesley Achitoff, p. 117; Lane Yerkes, pp. 118-127; Marian Ebert, pp. 128-129; Terry Fehr, pp. 130-133; Marian Ebert, pp. 134-139; Jan Pyk, pp. 140-149; Angela Fernan, pp. 154-157; Allen Eitzen, pp. 158-163; Renee Daily, pp. 164-171; Stan Skardinski, pp. 172-181; Lynn Cherry, pp. 182-191; Allen Eitzen, pp. 196-205; Marian Ebert, pp. 206-209; Will Harmuth, pp. 210-219; John Killgrew, pp. 220-226; Oni, pp. 227-237; Thomas Vroman, pp. 240-241; Albert Pucci, pp. 244-255; Yee Lin, pp. 256-267; Barbara McClintock, pp. 268-277; Terry Fehr, pp. 278-280; C. S. Ewing, pp. 288-296; Tom Newson, pp. 281-287.

Photo Credits: Ian Berry, Magnum, cover and p. 1; Marjorie Pickens, pp. 8-9; Peter Vadnai, E. P. A., p. 11; Ginger Chih, p. 12; Peter Vadnai, E. P. A., p. 13; Peter B. Kaplan, pp. 54-55; Jerry Stebbins, Webb Photos, pp. 104-105; Peter B. Kaplan, pp. 150-151; Dennis Stock, Magnum, pp. 194-195; Flip Schulke, Black Star, pp. 242-243.

D.C. HEATH AND COMPANY

Lexington, Massachusetts/Toronto, Ontario

ACKNOWLEDGMENTS

Every reasonable effort has been made to trace the owners of copyright materials in this book, but in some instances this has proven impossible. The publishers will be glad to receive information leading to more complete acknowledgments in subsequent printings of the book, and in the meantime extend their apologies for any omissions.

To Abingdon Press for "One for the Computo," adapted from *The Terrible Troubles of Rupert Piper* by Ethelyn Parkinson. Story copyright © 1959 by Abingdon Press.

To Michael Cooney for "Word of Mouth," adapted from "Underground School Songs," first published in the *American Red Cross Youth News,* Feb., 1974.

To Thomas Y. Crowell for "Company Clothes," from *In One Door and Out the Other* by Aileen Fisher. Copyright © 1969 by Aileen Fisher. By permission of Thomas Y. Crowell.

To Curtis Brown, Ltd. and Stephen Mooser for "Popcorn," "Basketballs and Bells," and "Su Ling's Arrow." Reprinted by permission of Curtis Brown, Ltd. and Stephen Mooser. Copyright © 1977.

To Delacorte Press for "Something Odd at the Ball Park," adapted from *Something Queer at the Ball Park* by Elizabeth Levy. Copyright © 1975 by Elizabeth Levy.

To Doubleday & Company, Inc. for "The Cat Sat on a Mat," from *A Necklace of Raindrops* by Joan Aiken. Copyright © 1968 by Joan Aiken. Reprinted by permission of Doubleday & Company, Inc.

To E.P. Dutton & Co., Inc. for "The Merry Menagerie," adapted from *Pets at the White House* by Carl Carmer. Copyright © 1952, 1962 by Carl Carmer. By permission of E.P. Dutton.

To Free to Be Foundation, Inc., for "My Dog Is a Plumber" by Dan Greenburg, from *Free to Be . . . You and Me,* published by McGraw-Hill. Copyright © 1972 Free to Be Foundation, Inc. Used by permission.

To William D. Hayes and Kathryn H. Hayes for "Use Your Head, Tom." Used by permission of the author and of Kathryn H. Hayes.

To Highlights for Children, Inc. for "The Search for the Mississippi" by Sharon Scott. Copyright © 1973 Highlights for Children, Inc., Columbus, Ohio; used and adapted by permission.

To Holt, Rinehart and Winston, Inc. for "Evan's Corner," adapted from *Evan's Corner* by Elizabeth Starr Hill. Copyright © 1967 by Elizabeth Starr Hill; for "Professor Coconut and the Thief," adapted from *Professor Coconut and the Thief* by Rita Golden Gelman and Joan Richter. Copyright © 1977 by Rita Golden Gelman and Joan Richter; and for three rhymes from *A Comparative Anthology of Children's Literature* by Mary Ann Nelson, copyright © 1972. All reprinted by permission of Holt, Rinehart and Winston, Publishers.

To King Features Syndicate, Inc. for two "Hi and Lois" strips. Copyright © 1971 by King Features.

To J. B. Lippincott Co. for "There Isn't Time." Copyright 1933, © renewed 1961 by Eleanor Farjeon. From *Poems for Children* by Eleanor Farjeon. Reprinted by permission of J. B. Lippincott Company.

To McGraw-Hill Book Company for "How Do We Know About Dinosaurs?" from *Discovering Dinosaurs* by Glenn O. Blough. Copyright © 1960 by Glenn O. Blough; and for "Heat Wave" from *Magical Storybook* by Jay Williams. Copyright © 1972 by Jay Williams. Both used with permission of McGraw-Hill Book Company.

To Thomas Nelson & Sons Ltd., London, for "Who's In?" by Elizabeth Fleming, from *The Creepie Stool.*

To Parents' Magazine Enterprises, Inc. for "The Tale of the Lazy Donkey" by Jill Palaez. Reprinted from *Humpty Dumpty's Magazine.* Copyright © 1966 by Parents' Magazine Enterprises, Inc.

To Plays, Inc. for "The Crystal Flask" by Karin Asbrand, reprinted by permission from *100 Plays for Children,* edited by A. S. Burack, Plays, Inc., Publishers. Copyright © 1945 by Plays, Inc. This play is for reading purposes only. For permission to produce this play, write to Plays, Inc., 8 Arlington St., Boston, MA 02116.

To Random House, Inc. for "Train Ride to Freedom," adapted by permission of Alfred A. Knopf, Inc., from Chapter 15 of "The Railroad to Freedom" from *Frederick Douglass: Slave-Fighter-Freeman* by Arna Bontemps. Copyright © 1959 by Arna Bontemps.

To Henry Regnery Co. for "The One in the Middle Is the Green Kangaroo" by Judy Blume. Copyright © 1969 by Judy Blume. Used by permission.

To The Saturday Evening Post Company for "Danger!" from *Danger in the Swamp* by D. J. Chaconas © 1966; for "The Fastest Car in the World" by Marjorie Kutchinski © 1965; for "The Great Wave" by Gail Tipperman Barclay © 1964; and for "The World's Best-Known Lamb" by Dorothy Sands Beers © 1968; all from *Jack and Jill* Magazine, copyright © 1966 by The Curtis Publishing Company. Reprinted by permission of the publisher.

To Scholastic Magazines, Inc. for "Los Muchachos—A Circus of Boys," adapted by permission of Scholastic Magazines, Inc., from *News Trails.* Copyright © 1974 by Scholastic Magazines, Inc.

To Scott, Foresman and Company for pronunciation key, grammatical key, and reduced key, from *Thorndike-Barnhart Intermediate Dictionary* by E. L. Thorndike and Clarence L. Barnhart. Copyright © 1974 by Scott, Foresman and Company. Reprinted by permission.

To William Jay Smith for "Laughing Time," from *Laughing Time,* published by Atlantic-Little, Brown, 1955, copyright © 1953, 1955 by William Jay Smith. Reprinted by permission of William Jay Smith.

Contents

one

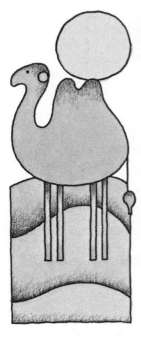

two

three

four

five

six

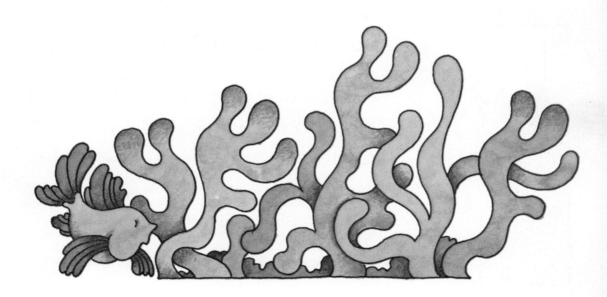

one

Shadow Song

My friend caught my shadow.
It didn't want to stay.
My friend caught my shadow
Before it ran away.
My friend caught my shadow
And slipped it right inside
The magic pocket of a line
Where sleeping shadows hide.

Bobbi Katz

13

Something Odd at the Ball Park

A strange person with a moustache stepped over Fletcher and knocked on Jill's back door. Fletcher was Jill's dog. He opened one eye but didn't move. He never moved unless he had to.

The strange person flashed a badge. "I just want to ask some questions," said the person.

"Hi, Gwen, what do you want?" asked Jill.

"How did you know it was me?"

"You're the only kid who has a moustache," said Jill.

Gwen took off her moustache and squeezed it back into her detective kit. "I'd like to watch you play baseball today," she said. "Let's go."

"Great," said Jill. "My dad just got me a new Rusty McGraw bat. I can't wait to use it."

Slam! Bang! With her new bat, Jill hit balls left and right. She was the star player of the Sparks that day.

About a week later, the coach gathered the team around him. "Our first game will be next Monday," said the coach, "and I'm going to give the lineup just before the game."

After the meeting, Jill said to Gwen, "Please help me look for my bat. I can't find it."

Gwen and Jill looked in the equipment room, under all the benches, and behind the water fountain. They looked all over, but found no bat.

Jill slammed her fist into her mitt. "It's my lucky bat. I'm no good without it."

The next day, Jill told the team that her bat was missing. She asked if anyone had seen it.

"Too bad, Jill," said Ben. "That's your lucky bat. I hope you find it."

"Tough luck," said Marshall.

"I didn't take it," said Erica.

Gwen stood listening and tap, tap, tapping on her braces. She always tapped her braces when she thought something odd was going on.

Gwen put on one of her funny noses. She crawled up behind Ben and tried to get a look at his bat. He turned around and stared at her.

"What are you doing?" Ben asked.

"Nothing," said Gwen, as she crawled away.

Next Gwen went up to Erica. "Why did you say you didn't take Jill's bat?" she asked.

"Because I didn't," said Erica.

"Maybe," said Gwen, tapping her braces as she walked toward Marshall.

"Why do you have on that funny-looking nose?" asked Marshall.

"Never mind," said Gwen.

On their way home, Gwen said to Jill, "Ben, Erica, and Marshall were the only ones who said anything when you asked about your bat. I think one of them took it. I've been doing some detective work."

"I don't think anybody stole my bat," said Jill. "I must have left it someplace. Stay out of it, please. You'll only get me in trouble."

Jill was right. The next day, Erica said, "Your friend thinks I took your bat. I didn't, and I don't think she should say things that aren't true."

"Yes," said Marshall. "She makes me angry."

The coach came up to Jill. "I've heard that your friend thinks a teammate stole your bat. Tell her to stay away from my team. A bat isn't that important. You just go on out there and do your best, Jill."

When Jill was alone, Gwen ran over, saying, "I know a way to trap the kid who stole your bat."

"Stop pretending to be a detective!" cried Jill. "This isn't a game. It's real. It's baseball."

And so, Gwen stopped coming to the ball park.

All week Jill tried every different bat the Sparks had. She just couldn't hit the ball the way she did with her Rusty McGraw bat.

Finally Jill went to see Gwen. "I'm sorry for all the things I said," she told Gwen.

"It's OK," said Gwen. "I knew you were upset. How is the baseball coming?"

"Awful," said Jill. "Tomorrow is the first game, and I bet I'm not in the lineup."

"I still think somebody stole your bat, and I could find out who," said Gwen. "I have a great plan. All we need is Fletcher and..." Gwen whispered her plan to Jill.

The next morning at the ball park, Jill walked around with a big smile. "I'm lucky to have my mitt," she said. "Maybe I lost my bat, but as long as I've got my mitt, I still feel lucky."

"That's the way to think," said the coach. "You're a good fielder. Don't worry about making the lineup. Just take it easy."

"Right," said Jill. "Just as long as I have my mitt." She walked over to Fletcher and scratched him as he lay on his back. When Jill got back up, she left her mitt beside her dog. Fletcher soon fell asleep in the warm sun.

Suddenly Fletcher's tail flew up. The dog jumped up as if someone had pulled his tail.

"It worked!" shouted Gwen from behind the bushes. "Jill, come quick! Someone stole your mitt! I think it's a boy, but I can't tell who."

They could just see the thief turn the corner on a bike. Gwen grabbed Fletcher. The two girls jumped on their bikes and rode after the thief as fast as they could.

"It's hopeless!" cried Jill. "Once he gets across Main Street, it's all downhill. We'll never catch up."

Ahead of them they could hear music. The boy was just reaching Main Street when a marching band turned the corner. The boy looked around and saw Gwen and Jill right behind him. He tried to dash across the street in front of the marchers.

Fletcher jumped up and sank his teeth into Jill's mitt, pulling the boy off his bike.

"It's Marshall!" shouted Jill.

"Get this dog off me!" cried Marshall.

"Not until you tell where Jill's lucky bat is," said Gwen.

"OK, OK," said Marshall. "I knew Jill was a better batter. I thought that without her lucky bat, I'd have a good chance to make the lineup. When she said her mitt was lucky, I thought I'd better take that too."

"The mitt was a trap!" said Gwen. "Jill tied it to Fletcher's tail with string from my detective kit."

"Now, where's my bat?" said Jill.

Marshall took them to his house. He had hidden the bat way in the back of his closet.

They retrieved it and hurried back to the ball park. The coach was so angry at Marshall that he didn't even let him play. Marshall had to be the water boy.

The coach picked Jill to play first base. She hit two home runs with her lucky Rusty McGraw bat. Gwen and Fletcher sat in the grandstand and cheered every time it was Jill's turn.

Gwen kept twisting in her seat and looking around.

"What are you looking for?" asked Marshall as he came by carrying two buckets of water.

"You never can tell when something odd may happen," said Gwen, "especially at a ball park!"

THINK ABOUT IT

1. How did Jill know the strange person at the door was Gwen?
2. What did Gwen think had happened to Jill's new bat?
3. Who finally caught the thief? What happened to the thief after he was caught?
4. Why did Jill think her bat was "lucky"?
5. What was Gwen's plan for trapping the thief?
6. How did Jill's teammates feel after Gwen questioned them about the missing bat?
7. Have you ever had something you thought of as "lucky"? Why did you feel that way?

THE MERRY MENAGERIE

Theodore Roosevelt was the 26th President of the United States, from 1901 – 1909. When he and his family lived in the White House, it overflowed with children and a menagerie of pets.

The Roosevelt family had six children. There was Alice, the oldest girl, who was a young lady when the family moved into the White House. There was Ted, the oldest boy, who spent much time away at school. And there were Kermit, Ethel, Archie, and Quentin.

The Roosevelt family also had many different animals. Important visitors to the White House were often surprised by some of the strange pets. Callers had to look carefully before sitting on a chair. A toad, a rabbit, or even a guinea pig might already be sitting there!

Back row: President and Mrs. Roosevelt. Middle row: Ethel, Alice, Quentin, Kermit, Archie. Front row: Ted.

The Roosevelt children were allowed to go everywhere in the White House, and they explored every corner with their menagerie of pets. The long halls and many large rooms became part of a noisy, happy playground.

The White House lawns also were part of the children's playground. In those days, many horses were kept on the grounds. All the Roosevelts were good riders, and each had a horse of his or her own.

Everyone's favorite was a frisky little pony named Algonquin. He really belonged to Archie, but all the children rode Algonquin. He loved to play. His favorite prank was to sneak up behind a child, lower his head, and push the child across the lawn.

Once, when Archie was ill, he longed to see his pony. Since he could not go outside, his younger brother, Quentin, brought the pony to him. Waiting for a time when no one was watching, Quentin led Algonquin into the cellar of the White House. He opened the elevator door, pushed the tiny pony in, and took him up to Archie's room.

Besides horses, there were many dogs in the Roosevelt menagerie. Some were big, some were little, but all were loved by the whole family.

Sailor Boy, a beautiful retriever, was the "boss" among the dogs. He took his job seriously, trying to make the other dogs behave. Sailor Boy got his name because he liked to go out with the children in their sailboat. If by chance Sailor Boy was ever left behind, he would often swim out to the boat so that he could be taken aboard.

A little black mutt named Skip was another obvious favorite with the whole family. Skip and Algonquin, the pony, became close friends. They had a game that they often played on the White House lawn.

Skip would lie quietly near the house, pretending to be asleep. Algonquin would gallop around the lawn. Then he would sneak up closer and closer to the dog.

Suddenly, as though by some previous signal, the pony would stop just for a second near the mutt. In that second, Skip would jump high in

the air and land on the pony's back. Then Algonquin would gallop away with Skip holding on and barking happily.

It often seemed that no one in the Roosevelt family could be serious for long. The White House was always filled with the sounds of children laughing, especially on rainy days when no one could play outside.

One of the favorite games the children played indoors was racing with Skip. A child would spread his or her legs, toss Skip backwards between them, and then dash for the end of the hall. The little mutt would run madly to catch up, sliding and scrambling on the slippery floors. Skip would often reach the end of the hall first.

When the children were away, the little mutt stuck close to their father. Skip sat on the President's lap throughout many an important and serious meeting.

Though Skip was very special to all the Roosevelts, there were other animals that were also quite special. Some of these were pets that many families would not allow in their homes.

The White House menagerie had birds, guinea pigs, and kittens. There was even a horned toad named Bill. And there were lots of snakes.

All the children loved snakes. Alice had a special favorite that she named Emily Spinach. The "Emily" was for Alice's Aunt Emily, who was very thin. "Spinach" was for the snake's green color.

Once Alice took Emily Spinach visiting, and the snake got lost in the living-room curtains. Later, it surprised Alice's friends by shedding its skin in another room.

Squirrels, rabbits, guinea pigs, ponies—all lived at the White House while Theodore Roosevelt was President. It is obvious that no living thing was too small or too large for the Roosevelt family to love. People have said that no previous President ever filled the White House with so many children, so many animals, and so much joy.

1. What is a *menagerie?*

2. What were some of the animals in the Roosevelt menagerie?

3. How did it happen that Algonquin, the pony, got into Archie's room?

4. What trick did Algonquin and Skip like to play?

5. Was the White House a happy place while the Roosevelts lived there? What makes you think as you do?

6. How did President Roosevelt feel about having all those animals around?

7. If you could have a menagerie, what animals would you choose to have in it?

3-D PICTURES

The pirate's treasure in this drawing looks almost real. So do some other objects in the picture. They look life-like because they stand away from the scene. To make a drawing seem alive, glue the important objects onto a background scene.

To make a 3-D picture, you'll need white construction paper, crayons or paints, thick cardboard, glue, and scissors. Read all of the directions before you start to work.

1. Color or paint a background scene on one sheet of construction paper. If you are drawing a treasure island, you might want to include sand, sky, and water. You can make a farm scene or a city picture rather than the treasure island, if you prefer.

2. On other sheets of construction paper, draw and color or paint the objects you want to be 3-D. They should be large, solid objects that will be easy to work with. When you are finished, carefully cut out each one.

3. Cut the cardboard into small pieces.

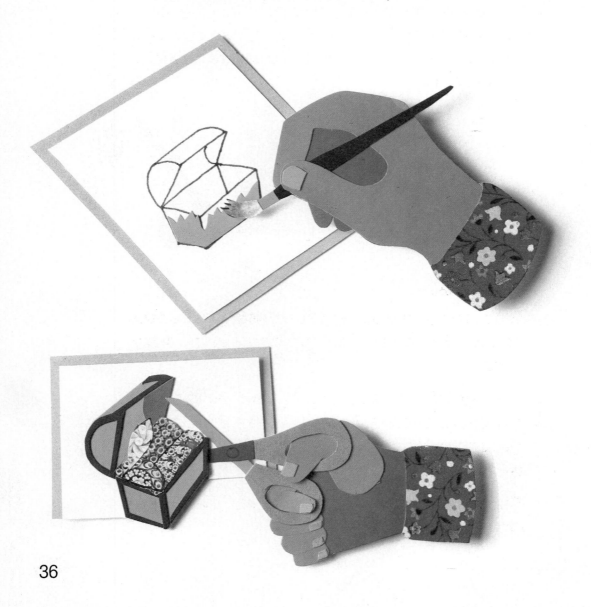

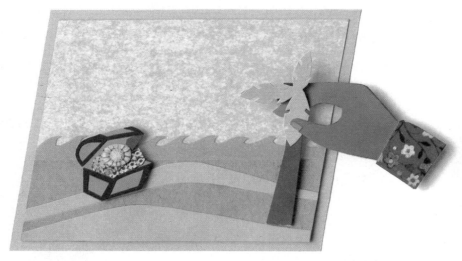

4. Glue two or three pieces of cardboard to the back of each 3-D object. Let the glue set for a few minutes.

5. Decide where each object belongs on your background scene. Then put a little glue on each piece of cardboard and glue the objects in place on the scene.

This is an easy and fun way to make your drawings come alive.

The Search for the Mississippi

Two French Explorers

Jacques Marquette moved closer to the warm campfire. The day had been long. His arms were terribly tired from many hours of paddling through the water in the little canoe. He could not even guess what might lie ahead on this trip into unknown land. Yet he felt happy. He and the other explorers were on their way at last!

"Well, Jacques, do you think we will find the river?" asked Louis Joliet, the leader of the explorers.

"If it is there, we will find it!"

Jacques Marquette and Louis Joliet were Frenchmen living in "New France." New France was a part of North America that was governed in those days by the country of France.

In the year 1673, the government of New France sent Marquette and Joliet exploring. They were to search for a river that led to the Pacific Ocean. The river lay somewhere southwest of New France, and the American Indians called it "Messipi." Those two facts were ALL the explorers really knew about the river.

But if anyone could find the Messipi, it would be these two. Jacques Marquette was a priest who could speak six American Indian languages. It was said that he could make friends with anyone he met. As for young Louis Joliet, he was already a well-known explorer.

Getting Ready for the Trip

The search for the river could not begin until the winter was over. While they waited for good weather, Marquette and Joliet had listened to stories about the Messipi. They had drawn maps of the course they would take—rough maps, made mostly from guesswork. They had bought the canoes and the supplies they would need.

They found five other Frenchmen who were willing to go with them. Then, at last, springtime came, and the journey started.

Into the Unknown

For a few days, the men paddled the two canoes in known waters. But they were not there for long. They were soon as deep into the wild as anyone who was not an American Indian had ever gone.

American Indian Guides

The explorers spent a night in an American Indian village. None of these Indians had ever seen the Messipi, but they knew that it lay to the west.

"Two of my people will take you to the place where the Fox River ends. After that, you must go on alone," the chief said.

With their guides, the explorers traveled along the Fox River as far as they could go. Then, carrying their canoes and supplies, the Frenchmen followed the Indians through the mud of a swamp. At last they reached the shore of still another river, the Wisconsin.

Rough Going

This was as far as their Indian guides would go. The Frenchmen were on their own now. Swiftly they reloaded the canoes and pushed off. Somewhere ahead, the unknown river ran.

It was slow, rough going down the Wisconsin River. There were many islands and sandbars. Several times a day, the canoes had to be carried to deeper water. Everyone struggled, growing wearier and wearier.

One day, the explorers saw a large river flowing south. "The Messipi!" shouted Joliet. "We have found the Messipi!"

Down the Great River

The water ran swift where the two rivers met. There were times of struggle and danger for the explorers and their light canoes. Then, at last, they were on the Messipi, or the Mississippi, riding gently on its slow-moving waters.

Day by day, their joy grew. Rolling hills gave way to prairie grass. In some places, the grass was taller than a person. Deer and buffalo were plentiful on the prairies and along the shore. Ducks and other birds shared the water with the two canoes.

The Gift of the Peace Pipe

There was no sign of Indians for some days after the canoes entered the Mississippi. The explorers seemed alone in a new world. One day, however, someone spotted a dark streak in the prairie grass. Was it a trail?

The canoes drew near the shore. Yes! There were tracks here. The dark streak turned out to be an Illinois Indian trail, and it was well-used.

Marquette and Joliet stepped from their canoe. They wanted to talk to the Indians who had made this trail.

A walk of many miles inland brought them to an Illinois Indian village. The chief and his people made the Frenchmen welcome and told what they knew of the great river. They fed their visitors roast buffalo and gave them a peace pipe to carry with them.

"It will be a sign to others that you come in peace," the chief said.

As the journey continued, the Frenchmen discovered that the chief was right. At least once, the peace pipe saved the lives of the whole party.

A Last Discovery

The days grew warmer as the explorers continued to follow the river southward. The countryside changed and changed again. The Mississippi grew wider and deeper as the waters of other rivers flowed into it.

The summer was more than half gone. Joliet and Marquette both knew that they should turn back soon. They must return home before the winter set in. Yet they went onward a while longer, seeking to discover still more facts.

At last came a day of important news. The explorers learned from some Indians that the river flowed south until it met the sea. At that place, the Indians said, a great many people had settled.

The Frenchmen looked at one another. There were settlers where the river met the sea! Swiftly Marquette and Joliet took in the meaning of those words. The "sea" to the south would have to be the Gulf of Mexico. So the Messipi, or Mississippi, flowed clear to the Gulf, not to the Pacific!

That part of North America was governed by Spain. The people who lived there must be Spanish settlers. Frenchmen would not be welcome there, for the governments of France and Spain were not very friendly just then.

Back Home Again

On the morning of July 17, the explorers headed back to New France. The men paddled hard. They had a long, long way to go. They could not allow themselves to be stuck in this wild land when winter came.

45

Two months later, the Messipi explorers came home. Marquette and Joliet had not done what they had set out to do. They had not found a way to the Pacific. But they had risked their lives to explore the great Mississippi and had learned much about the river. Within just a few years, settlers began moving into the Mississippi valley, with its plentiful wildlife and wide open spaces.

Louis Joliet and Jacques Marquette were French Canadians, but today they are heroes of the United States. Their discovery opened the way for the western part of this country to be settled.

THINK ABOUT IT

1. Who were Jacques Marquette and Louis Joliet?

2. What had these two men been sent to explore? Why?

3. How did American Indians help the explorers?

4. What did Marquette and Joliet find out about the Messipi River?

5. Why didn't Marquette and Joliet follow the river to the Gulf of Mexico?

6. Why do you think explorers are willing to take risks? Would you be willing to take a risk to try to discover something important?

7. How are space explorers today like the people who explored America long ago?

47

Los Muchachos

The stage lights go on. The audience at the circus stops talking. There, on a high wire strung across the stage, stands a boy. He is ready to begin his act — walking across the wire.

The audience is hushed. Will the boy make it across the wire without falling?

The boy holds a long pole to help him balance. Slowly, carefully, he steps along the wire. A few times, the boy leans a little to one side, then to the other. He looks shaky. Will he fall? No! He straightens up and stands steady again. He makes it safely across the wire, and the once hushed audience now cheers.

The boy is José Cabreas. He is a member of a Spanish circus called "Los Muchachos" — "The Boys." They have made many tours to bring the circus to people in other lands.

When the boys are not on tour, they live in a special town of their own — Bemposta, in Spain. They study at the circus school there.

That circus school isn't easy! The boys work on the skills they need in their acts for about four hours every day. They also work on their school lessons. Even when they go on tour, Los Muchachos must do their schoolwork, for teachers travel with them.

Exciting things often happen in circuses, and the Los Muchachos circus is no different. The boys of this circus have learned something important that every good performer knows. Hard work can make exciting things happen. The audience, watching, may think, "How brave that performer is! He makes it look so easy!"

The performer knows that he does well mostly because he has had good training. Suppose you were a boy like José Cabreas, with a high-wire act. Your training would teach you the best way to use your feet and toes to safely cross the wire strung high above the ground. You would learn the best way to breathe and to use the pole for balance. Many other skills would be a part of your training.

Then you would practice your act — and practice — and *practice!*

Do the boys in the circus sometimes become shaky about doing their acts? Are there days when they'd rather not perform at all? Maybe, but they go on anyway. If you were in the audience, you could not tell for sure how they felt inside. Indeed, as you watched them, you might be more upset than they!

The members of this Spanish circus are happy. They like living and working and touring together. If you were to ask them about their way of life, they would be likely to say, "Los Muchachos is really an exciting circus act. We are very happy in Bemposta. We're just like a big, happy family."

1. What kind of circus is Los Muchachos?

2. How do the boys who perform in this circus get to be so good?

3. Do you think there are days when some of the boys would rather not perform at all?

4. How are the boys in the circus like "a big, happy family"?

5. Do you think being part of a circus would be a hard life? Why or why not? What would you like best about it? What would you like least?

Company Clothes

I had to dress up
and not wear jeans
or even my comfortable
in-betweens,
and not wear boots
or my zebra sweater
because Mother said
she'd had a letter
and someone she knew
when she was small
was stopping to call
so I had to look better.

And what do you know!
Their boy was John . . .
and he had jeans
and a sweater on!
So I changed mine back
in one-two-three,
to keep my company
company.

Aileen Fisher

two

The Great Wave

The islands of Hawaii were formed long ago by great volcanoes. Time and again, hot lava spilled out of these volcanoes and into the sea. After many years, a group of islands appeared above the water.

All the mountains on these islands were also formed by the lava that spilled from the volcanoes. As the hot lava cooled, it became black and hard. Even today, the mountains in Hawaii are steep and have many sharp places.

Lili and her family lived in a small village near the beach at the foot of one of the lava mountains in Hawaii. The people of the village fished for a living. Most days they spent fishing in the ocean, but sometimes they traveled into town to sell the fish they had caught.

One summer morning Lili's father and brothers left for town to sell their catch from the day before. Lili's mother left to do some shopping for the family. Lili took some fish outside to the beach and sat down on a rock to clean them for dinner that night. But instead of cleaning fish, she stared out at the wide blue ocean that lapped the shores of Hawaii.

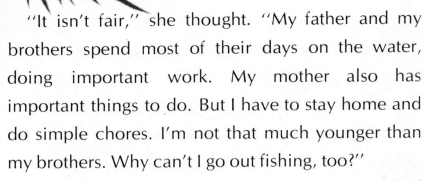

"It isn't fair," she thought. "My father and my brothers spend most of their days on the water, doing important work. My mother also has important things to do. But I have to stay home and do simple chores. I'm not that much younger than my brothers. Why can't I go out fishing, too?"

Lili looked at her little sister, Puhuka, who had come out to the beach with her. Puhuka was playing at the water's edge. Lili had to keep her out of trouble while their mother was away. "That's all anyone thinks I can do. Well, someday I'll show everyone that I can do other things, too," Lili

thought. She sighed a loud sigh and began to clean the fish. "One day I won't be spending my time this way."

Even before she looked up, Lili could feel that there was something wrong. There was a silence in the air. She lifted her eyes from the fish and looked for Puhuka. But Puhuka was all right. Lili looked beyond her little sister to the sea.

The sea! Lili's eyes grew wide and her mouth dropped open. The half-cleaned fish fell to the sand. She couldn't believe what her eyes were telling her.

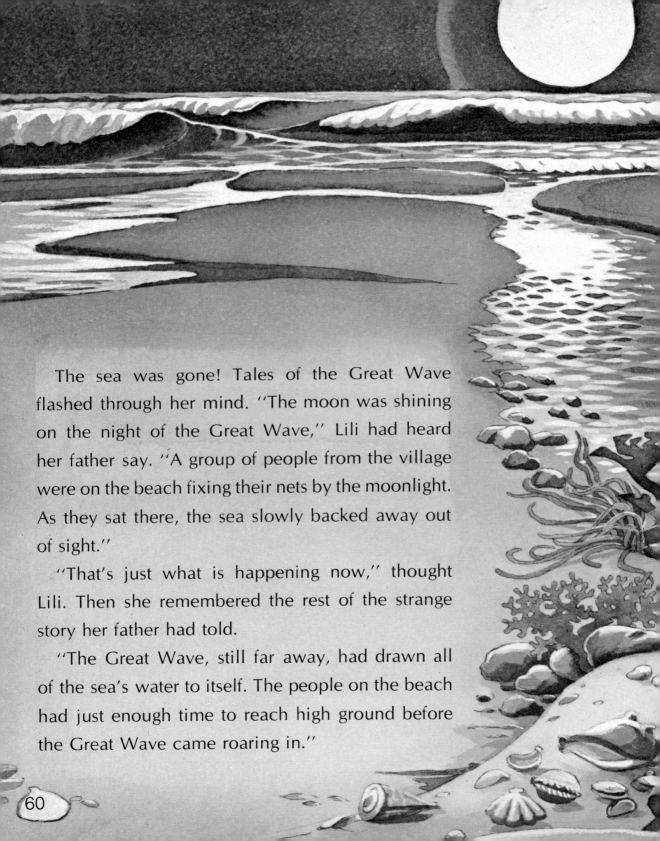

The sea was gone! Tales of the Great Wave flashed through her mind. "The moon was shining on the night of the Great Wave," Lili had heard her father say. "A group of people from the village were on the beach fixing their nets by the moonlight. As they sat there, the sea slowly backed away out of sight."

"That's just what is happening now," thought Lili. Then she remembered the rest of the strange story her father had told.

"The Great Wave, still far away, had drawn all of the sea's water to itself. The people on the beach had just enough time to reach high ground before the Great Wave came roaring in."

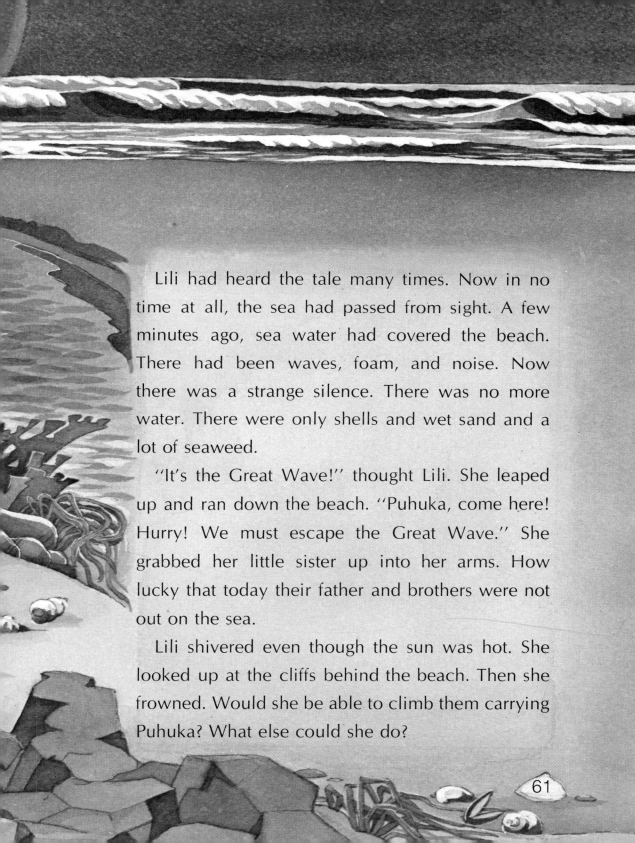

Lili had heard the tale many times. Now in no time at all, the sea had passed from sight. A few minutes ago, sea water had covered the beach. There had been waves, foam, and noise. Now there was a strange silence. There was no more water. There were only shells and wet sand and a lot of seaweed.

"It's the Great Wave!" thought Lili. She leaped up and ran down the beach. "Puhuka, come here! Hurry! We must escape the Great Wave." She grabbed her little sister up into her arms. How lucky that today their father and brothers were not out on the sea.

Lili shivered even though the sun was hot. She looked up at the cliffs behind the beach. Then she frowned. Would she be able to climb them carrying Puhuka? What else could she do?

When the Great Wave rolled in across the beach, the only safe place would be high up on the steep cliffs. She could not misjudge anything if she and Puhuka were going to reach safety. Lili raced across the beach to the base of the steepest cliff.

Grabbing a piece of fishing net, Lili made it into a sling. She put Puhuka in the sling and tied it around her neck. Puhuka clung tightly to Lili. Then Lili started to climb the side of the sharp lava cliff. Before she had gone very far, her hands and feet were cut and bleeding.

Lili climbed and climbed until she was so out of breath that she could climb no farther. She pressed her body close against the hard lava to rest for a minute. Her heart was pounding so hard that she could feel every beat.

Without moving her body, Lili turned her head and looked over her shoulder. Once again, she could not believe what her eyes told her. Now she saw a single silvery blue wall of water that stretched up higher and higher. It seemed to Lili that the water was taller than the mountains, taller even than the sky itself.

The wall of water was moving toward the beach. Lili had never thought that there could be so much water in a single wave.

The silence was gone now. Instead, a strange angry, roaring sound came to her ears. Lili shivered. She had not climbed high enough. "Is there still time?" she thought, beginning to climb again. The roar grew louder. Lili did not dare to look back. The wave was almost upon them.

Lili's foot slipped on a loose rock. She had misjudged her step. Her hands clawed at the cliff. Puhuka screamed. Lili pressed tightly against the side of the cliff. The sharp rock cut into her face and body, but her hands and feet found a grip. Unless she slipped again, they would be safe.

Above them, the side of the cliff was straight. Lili could go no farther. Shivering with cold and fear, she clung to the cliff and looked back.

Far below them, the Great Wave rolled over the beach. Three fishing boats lying by the shore were quickly swallowed. The wave roared on, and the rock where Lili had been sitting was suddenly

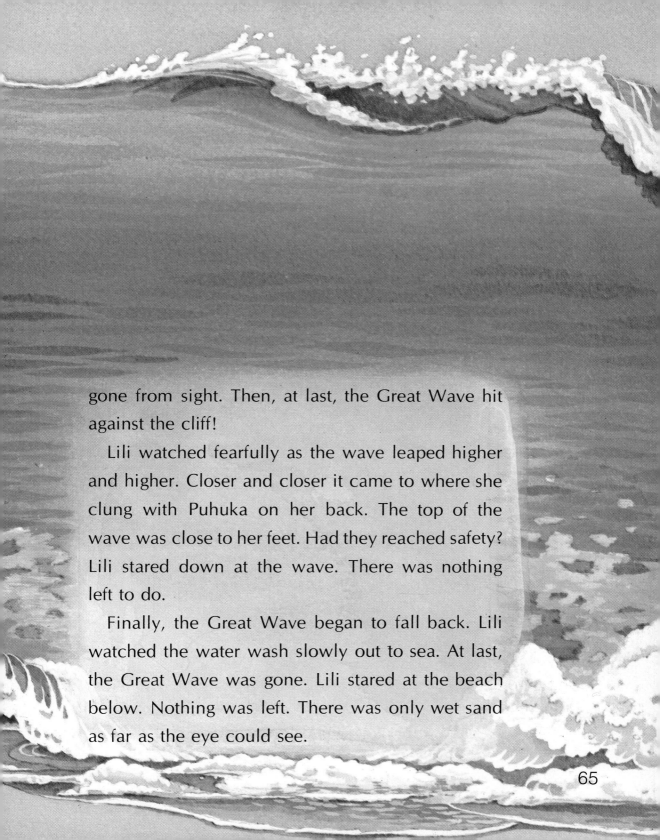

gone from sight. Then, at last, the Great Wave hit against the cliff!

Lili watched fearfully as the wave leaped higher and higher. Closer and closer it came to where she clung with Puhuka on her back. The top of the wave was close to her feet. Had they reached safety? Lili stared down at the wave. There was nothing left to do.

Finally, the Great Wave began to fall back. Lili watched the water wash slowly out to sea. At last, the Great Wave was gone. Lili stared at the beach below. Nothing was left. There was only wet sand as far as the eye could see.

It was over. Lili loosened her grip and began to make her way back down the cliff. Their mother came running across the beach. When Lili and Puhuka reached the ground, she flung her arms around them.

"Lili! And my little Puhuka!" Mama was saying. "You are indeed brave, Lili! Because of you, we are all safe. Tonight I shall speak to your father. You have shown that you are grown-up enough to help your brothers on the fishing boat."

Lili looked longingly out at the wide blue ocean. "Fishing," she thought. She stared down at her bleeding hands. Then she reached around and lifted Puhuka from her tired back. She had not wasted her time *this* morning!

Lili smiled at her mother. "Oh," she said, 'I'll be glad to fish. But my job here is important, too."

From the proud, happy look on her mother's face, Lili knew she was right.

THINK ABOUT IT

1. At the start of the story, Lili is feeling sorry for herself. Why?

2. When Lili saw that the sea was gone, what did she think of?

3. How did Lili and her sister escape the Great Wave?

4. After the Great Wave, how did Lili feel about her tasks at home? How did she feel about going fishing with her father and brothers?

5. Do you agree with the way Lili felt at the end of the story?

6. Have you ever had to act quickly in face of danger? What did you do? Why is it so important to think clearly and act quickly at such a time?

The Crystal Flask

by *Karin Asbrand*

CHARACTERS

Princess Lilita

First Fairy Godmother

The King

The Queen

Second Fairy Godmother

Prince Sigwald

Cara, a Lady-in-Waiting

A Nurse

SCENE I

SETTING: *A throne room in a palace. The King and the Queen are seated on their thrones. A nurse holds the Princess Lilita. The fairy godmothers stand on either side of her.*

First Godmother: To my godchild, I give this silver flask. It is filled with laughter. Keep it lightly corked so that Lilita's laughter may overflow and stay with her always. *(She hands flask to King.)*

King: I thank you.

Second Godmother: I, too, have a gift for my godchild. This crystal flask is full of tears — Lilita's tears, which she must someday shed.

Queen: Tears? No, the Princess must never know the meaning of either tears or sorrow. We will keep this flask tightly corked and hide it.

Second Godmother: There is no joy that is not greater for having shed a tear or two. But the gift is hers. Do with it whatever pleases you. *(She hands flask to Queen.)*

Queen: It is indeed a beautiful flask, but we must hide it.

First Godmother (*Kisses baby*): And so farewell. May your gay laughter ring throughout the palace for many a day.

Second Godmother (*Kisses baby*): I, too, must say farewell. Someday you will find that even tears will bring you happiness. (*Godmothers leave.*)

Queen: Let's put this flask of tears upon the highest shelf.

King: Quite right, my dear. We'll hide it now before a single tear escapes. (*King and Queen and nurse with baby leave.*)

71

SCENE II

SETTING: *The same throne room, sixteen years later. The nurse and Cara, one of the Queen's Ladies-in-Waiting, stand in the middle of the room.*

Cara: I am growing very tired of hearing the Princess laugh. It seems to me that she has done nothing else for sixteen years.

Nurse: She has always laughed at everybody and everything. If I knew where they had hidden the crystal flask, I would get it and pull out the stopper.

Cara: The King and Queen would punish you.

Nurse: Who cares if I am punished? I love the Princess very much, but her feelings are all bottled up. Everyone needs to cry sometimes.

Cara: I know where the crystal flask is hidden. I was the one who climbed up on the ladder and hid it. But I would never dare tell anyone. Hush! Here comes the Princess now. *(Princess Lilita enters, laughing.)*

Nurse: Well, what is so funny?

Princess: Oh, don't mind me. You know that I am always laughing. I wish I could stop, but unless I find the crystal flask, I can't. If only I could cry just once.

Cara: I know where the crystal flask is hidden, Princess Lilita. I should know. *I* hid it.

Princess: Please tell me where it is. I will reward you well.

Cara: Come, we'll get a ladder. You shall have your crystal flask. *(They leave. King and Queen enter.)*

King: For all our care, I don't believe that Lilita is happy.

Queen: She never cries.

King: But perhaps a few tears never really hurt anyone, my dear. Perhaps we should give the crystal flask to her. To think that she has never shed a tear in all her life!

Queen: And she never shall shed one, if I can help it. *(Princess Lilita enters, carrying the crystal flask and crying. There is no stopper on the flask. She is followed by the nurse and Cara.)*

Queen: The crystal flask! Who has done this terrible thing to my child?

Cara: The Princess climbed up on the ladder herself, but when she was halfway down, she took the stopper out and dropped it.

Nurse: Her pet dog took the stopper in his mouth and ran with it into the garden.

Cara: None of us can find it.

Princess: And I cannot stop crying!

King: We must find the stopper at once. Post notices throughout the land. Whoever retrieves the stopper to the flask may ask of me any wish, and I will grant it.

SCENE III

SETTING: *The same throne room, two weeks later. The King and Queen are seated on their thrones.*

King: Fourteen days have now gone by, and the stopper still has not been found. *(Prince Sigwald enters.)* What are we going to do?

Prince: I think I can help, Your Majesty. I am your neighbor, Prince Sigwald. *(He holds up the stopper for the crystal flask.)* Is this what you have been seeking?

Queen: It is, indeed!

King: I will send for the Princess so that we may stop her tears and bring laughter into her life again. *(He rings a bell. Cara enters.)*

Cara: Did you call for me, your Majesty?

King: Yes. Take the stopper to the crystal flask and put it on tightly. Then bring the Princess here. *(Cara leaves.)* And now, Prince, tell me your wish, and I shall grant it.

Prince: Your Majesty, I wish to wed the Princess Lilita when she turns nineteen.

King: That *I* cannot grant you! You must ask the Princess if she wishes to wed you. *(Princess enters. He turns to Lilita.)* My dear, this is our neighbor, Prince Sigwald. He has found the stopper to the crystal flask, and in return, he has asked to marry you. *(Princess smiles.)* It makes me so happy to see you smiling again!

Princess: I feel so lighthearted and gay. I think my tears have washed away my troubles. *(Turns to Sigwald)* Thank you for returning the stopper. I cannot yet say if I will marry you, but I certainly would like to be friends. *(She smiles and takes his arm.)*

Queen: Well, now we must hide that crystal flask where it can never be found again.

Princess: No, Mother, give it to me. My happiness now is greater because I have shed some tears.

Queen: The Fairy Godmother said you would find that to be true.

Princess: Side by side I will keep these flasks — the silver flask of laughter and the crystal one of tears. Surely, I will be a better ruler if I can weep with my people. But I will take care that my tears and theirs will be few.

King: Well said. May you someday rule, both wisely and well.

THINK ABOUT IT

1. Why did the Second Godmother choose a flask of tears as a gift for Princess Lilita?

2. Why, sixteen years later, did Princess Lilita want the flask of tears?

3. What terrible thing happened when the flask of tears was finally found?

4. When the Prince found the stopper, the King did NOT grant him his wish. Why not? How did the Prince feel about this?

5. Did you agree with the Princess when she said, "Surely, I will be a better ruler if I can weep with my people"? Why or why not?

HAVE SOME FUN

When cartoons are used to tell a story, they almost always have more than one panel. This kind of cartoon story is called a comic strip.

Read the comic strip on this page about Dot and her younger sister, Trixie. How many panels are there? Does the strip use balloons to show that the characters are speaking?

Look at the balloons used for Trixie and Dot. How are they different? Since Trixie is a baby and cannot talk, her balloon is used to show what she is thinking.

In the following comic strip Trixie is again drawing, and she is thinking as she draws. Her balloons have been left empty for you to fill in your own ideas. Use the picture clues to help you decide what Trixie is thinking.

If you would like to know what Trixie was really thinking, turn to page 255.

Your group should start to plan a cartoon story at least 16 panels long. Decide who your characters will be. Where will they go? What will they do? What will they say?

Sketch each panel on a sheet of paper. Remember, only one thing should take place in a panel. You might want to save the sketches for use with "A Homemade Television Set", which is next in your book.

A HOMEMADE TELEVISION SET

Do you like to watch television? A television set is a very expensive machine. Your group can make something like it that isn't nearly as expensive. You can use your cartoon ideas from the previous article to make a filmstrip for your television show.

To make a television set you'll need: a large box, a roll of shelf paper, a ruler, crayons, and scissors. Your group should read and discuss all of the directions before you begin to work. You may want to choose different people for each job.

1 Remove the flaps from the top of the box.

2 Cut slits, 1/2 inch from the open end, on two opposite sides of the box. The length of the slits should be a little wider than your paper. Then you will be able to pull the paper through the slits.

3 To make the filmstrip, roll the paper out to the length you need for your story. Mark the paper into squares the size of your box.

4 Allow each person in your group to draw several panels of your cartoon. Do not draw in the first square. Print the words in balloons or use captions at the bottom of each picture to tell about the action. Use a black crayon to darken the print so that your viewers will be able to read it. Then roll up your filmstrip.

5 Place the box on a desk so that the slits are at the top and bottom. Pull the end of the filmstrip through the top and bottom slits. Pull only as far as the first square.

Now you are ready to have a cartoon show. Pull the filmstrip slowly from the bottom. Stop at each panel to allow the viewers time to read. You could show your cartoon for the rest of your class to enjoy. Maybe another class in your school would enjoy seeing it, too.

HOW DO WE KNOW ABOUT DINOSAURS?

Dinosaur is the name used for many different kinds of animals that roamed the Earth many, many years ago. There are no written records of what these animals looked like. But scientists have ways of discovering facts about dinosaurs.

How do we know that they lived? The dinosaurs themselves left records that scientists call "fossils." Fossils are traces left by plants or animals that lived in the past. They took a very long time to form. Dinosaurs left teeth and bones and even footprints as records of themselves.

In 1811, a twelve-year-old English girl made one of the first important dinosaur fossil discoveries. Mary Anning collected shells and bones that she found on the beaches and cliffs near her house. One day, after a big rain, Mary found the skeleton of an animal that had lived in the sea. Nothing like it had ever been seen before, and scientists came from all over England to study it.

More fossils were found in England in 1822 by Dr. and Mrs. Gideon Mantell. Mrs. Mantell discovered a rock with a large tooth in it lying by the side of the road near their home. Dr. Mantell collected fossils, so she saved her discovery to show to him. He returned to the spot and found several more of the strange teeth, along with some fossil bones. Scientists were very excited about the Mantells' find. The teeth and bones were the first clues they had to the fact that enormous animals had lived on land long ago.

Another important clue was discovered in 1922. While hunting for fossils, a group of scientists found fossil dinosaur eggs. Some of the eggs even had tiny fossil dinosaurs inside them! Until these eggs were found, scientists were not sure how dinosaurs gave birth to their young.

Most dinosaur fossils were formed in one of three ways. When a dinosaur died, it was often washed into the water of rivers or seas. Because of its weight, it settled to the bottom, where mud, clay, and sand soon covered it. Most parts of the dinosaur rotted. But the bones, which were hard, did not rot.

Many, many years went by. The bones continued to be covered by more and more mud, clay, and sand, which slowly turned to rock. As the rock hardened, it formed a mold for the dinosaur bones and slowly became a fossil. This kind of fossil is a *mold*.

Another kind of fossil was made when the dinosaur bones themselves turned into stone. All bones have many tiny holes in them. For a very long time, water moved through the holes in the dinosaur bones that lay at the bottom of rivers and seas. The water left tiny pieces of minerals behind. Little by little, the holes were filled with the minerals, causing the bones to turn into stone. When this happens, we say that the bones are *petrified*.

The third kind of fossil is a *print.* Sometimes, a dinosaur left a track in soft mud. Often, other animals would walk across the print and spoil it. But sometimes sand would wash into the footprint and fill it. When the mud under the sand hardened, it formed a fossil of the dinosaur track. Many dinosaur prints have been found in the Connecticut River Valley.

As years passed, the earth changed, and many rivers and seas dried up. The mold fossils and the petrified fossils that had formed under water were then on dry, rocky land. Not until then could anyone dig them up.

Scientists have learned where to look for fossils. Very hard rocks almost never contain fossils. Rocks that are not so hard were formed mostly from mud, sand, or clay. These rocks are far more likely to have fossils inside them.

When scientists begin a search for fossils, they may find just a few small ones—tiny bones or teeth. They may find only bone chips. Sometimes they may discover what looks like a small bone sticking out of a rock. If they chip away some of the rock, they may find that the bone is not so small after all. It may turn out to be an enormous bone or many small bones. It may even turn out to be a whole group of bones that can be fitted together to make a dinosaur skeleton.

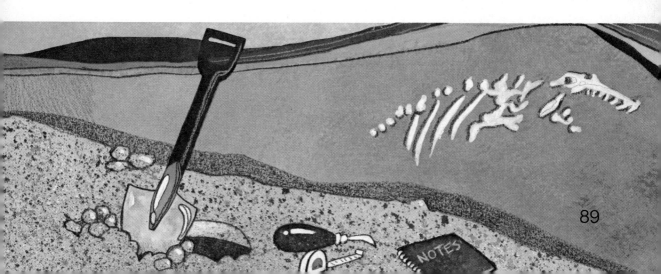

Scientists will often take their discoveries back to their lab to continue working on them. Sometimes the bones fit together into a skeleton just as they come from the rock. More often they do not. Then the scientists must fit the bones together the way you fit the parts of a puzzle together. Facts they have already gathered from other dinosaur fossils help them to connect the bones.

Sometimes the scientists find that the bones they have discovered will not make a skeleton at all. Other times they discover that some of these bones will connect with other bones found in another place at another time.

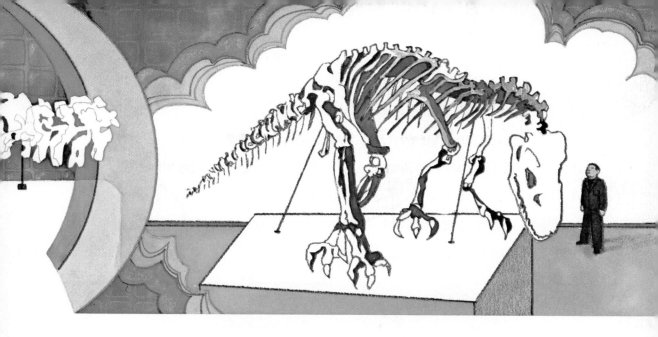

By gathering bones from many different places, scientists have been able to connect whole dinosaur skeletons. This takes many years of slow, careful digging and lab work. In fact, it can take scientists as long as fifty years to put together a whole dinosaur.

Dinosaur fossils have helped scientists learn many facts about the animals that roamed the earth so long ago. The fossils can tell people how big and how strong the animals were. By studying the shapes of the fossil bones, scientists can see how the bones were joined together and how the muscles worked. This also helps them to know how the skeleton, itself, looked.

Fossils of dinosaur tracks help scientists to tell how dinosaurs walked. These prints also tell about the weight and size of the animals.

Scientists have also found fossil prints of dinosaur skin. These prints help them to learn something about how the outside of a live dinosaur looked.

Fossils are still being found today, and not only by scientists. Workers who are building roads sometimes find them. Builders who are digging the ground for new houses sometimes find them. People on vacation discover them in cliffs along the beach. Who knows? There may even be fossils deep in the ground near you!

THINK ABOUT IT

1. What is a fossil?

2. What kinds of fossils have dinosaurs left?

3. What important fossil discovery did Mary Anning make? What discovery did Dr. and Mrs. Mantell make?

4. By studying fossils, what have scientists been able to find out about dinosaurs?

5. How is putting together a dinosaur skeleton like putting together a puzzle? Which is harder? Why?

6. Would you like to be a scientist who works with fossils? Why or why not?

The Cat
Sat on the Mat

The cat sat on the mat. Lots of cats do that, everyone knows. And nothing strange comes of it. But once a cat sat on a mat and something strange did come of it.

There was once a little girl called Emma Pippin. She lived with her Aunt Lou. They were very poor, too poor to buy a house, so they lived in an old bus.

It stood by a high white wall. Inside this wall were many lovely green apple trees, on which were growing many lovely red apples. The apple trees were owned by a proud man called Sir Laxton Superb.

Every day Aunt Lou went through a door in the wall to work for Sir Laxton Superb. Aunt Lou picked the apples. But she could not take any lovely red apples for herself. Sir Laxton Superb was a very mean man. He let her take only the apples that were going bad. And he only paid her a dime a day.

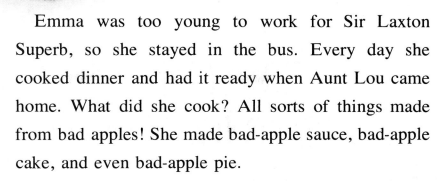

Emma was too young to work for Sir Laxton Superb, so she stayed in the bus. Every day she cooked dinner and had it ready when Aunt Lou came home. What did she cook? All sorts of things made from bad apples! She made bad-apple sauce, bad-apple cake, and even bad-apple pie.

Now Emma was growing very fast. She was growing so fast that soon she would be too big for her one and only dress.

"If we take your dress off to wash it," Aunt Lou said, "you may not be able to get it back on. I shall wash you and your dress both together."

So Aunt Lou put Emma in the tub, washed Emma and the dress, and hung them both on the line to dry.

As Emma was swinging in the wind, a poor old fairy came along. When she saw Emma swinging on the line, she started to laugh. She laughed and she laughed! She laughed so much she nearly fell over!

"Oh!" she said when she could stop laughing. "I have never seen anyone hanging on a line before. You can't think how funny you look!" Then she told Emma, "You have cheered me up, so I shall try

to help you. I am too old and poor to give you a big present. But I will give you three of my dresses."

So the fairy gave Emma three dresses, one red, one blue, and one gray. "And as well as the dresses," she said, "I will give you a kitten to play with." The kitten was called Sam, and he was black with green eyes.

Aunt Lou cut up the red dress and the blue dress and made new dresses for Emma. They looked beautiful.

Emma made a gray mat from the fairy's gray dress and put it on her bed. Sam jumped onto it. But on his way, he walked over her pillow and left black footprints before sitting on the mat.

"Oh dear, Sam," said Emma. "I *wish* you would clean your feet on your mat."

Sam stood up and looked at Emma. Then he cleaned his feet on the mat! Emma *was* surprised.

"Why!" she said. "It must be a wishing mat. What else can I wish? I wish I had a big chicken pie and some ice cream for Aunt Lou's dinner."

Just as Emma said this, Sam got up. And as Emma said *ice,* Sam jumped off his mat.

When Emma looked on the kitchen table, there was a big chicken pie and a lump of ice.

"I wished for ice cream, not ice," said Emma. "I wish the ice would turn into ice cream."

But the ice did not turn into ice cream.

Emma came to a conclusion. "I know," she said. "The mat is only a wishing mat when Sam is sitting on it. Please, Sam, will you get back on your mat?" But Sam wanted to go out, and he jumped out of the window.

Next morning, when Sam came home, he jumped up onto his mat. Emma had been waiting for this.

"I wish I had some toys!" she said. "A jump rope! And some balloons! And a ball!"

All the things were there that Emma had wished for. It was a very happy occasion. Emma and Sam played all day. At last they were both tired. Sam went to sleep on his mat.

"I wish I had a paint box!" Emma said. At once, there was a big, lovely paint box on the table.

"Oh, what lovely paints!" Emma said. "I shall paint a fine picture. Now, where shall I paint it? I know!" she said. "I'll paint on the white wall."

So she painted a picture on Sir Laxton Superb's high white wall. It was a very fine picture — the finest in the whole world.

And all the time, Sam went on sleeping on his mat. He was tired out.

Then Aunt Lou came through the door in the wall. After Aunt Lou came Sir Laxton Superb. Sir Laxton Superb saw the picture. And his face went red — redder than the reddest apple you ever saw!

"*What* have you done to my lovely white wall?" he said. He looked so cross that Emma thought he might go off — bang — like a balloon.

99

"I've painted the best picture in the whole world on it," she said. "Aren't you pleased?"

But Sir Laxton Superb was not pleased. He was not at all pleased!

"You must rub it all off again!" he said. "And you must leave *at once! Today!*"

Aunt Lou began to cry. "But where can we go?" she said.

"I don't care!" Sir Laxton Superb said. "I wish the wind would blow you and your old bus up into the sky!"

And Sam was *still* asleep on his mat!

That very minute a great wind blew Aunt Lou and Emma and the bus up into the air. Up they went, up, up, and up, till they landed on a fat white cloud.

"Well!" said Aunt Lou. "I thought of living in plenty of places, but I never thought of living up in the sky! What shall we find to eat up here?"

"That's easy," Emma said. And she wished for a roast chicken and a bottle of milk. For Sam was still asleep on his mat!

And they found lots of apples — because the wind had blown all of the apples off Sir Laxton Superb's trees. They were rolling about, all over the sky!

From that day on, Sir Laxton Superb's trees never had any more apples.

If you look up some dark night, you may see the old bus shining away up there. And you are almost sure to see some of the apples.

1. Where did Emma Pippin and her Aunt Lou live? Why did they live there?

2. Who owned the apple trees that grew on the other side of the high white wall? What kind of person was he?

3. Why did Aunt Lou decide to wash Emma's dress with Emma in it?

4. How did Emma find out that the gray mat was a wishing mat?

5. Once Emma found out about the mat, what kinds of wishes did she make?

6. Did the wishing mat work for anyone besides Emma? How do you know?

7. How might Emma and Aunt Lou have come down from the sky? Why do you think they decided to stay up in the sky?

WHO'S IN?

"The door is shut fast
And everyone's out."
But people don't know
What they're talking about!
Say the fly on the wall,
And the flame on the coals,
And the dog on his rug,
And the mice in their holes,
And the kitten curled up,
And the spiders that spin—
"What, everyone out?
Why, everyone's in!"

Elizabeth Fleming

103

three

The Story Teller

Pedro's mind never rested. He was a small boy with large ideas about the world and himself.

Pedro's papa thought he knew what the trouble was. The small town in which they lived was a well-known tourist town. It was in a state that used to be a part of Mexico. People came from all over to see the old adobe houses. These earthen, adobe buildings were perhaps the oldest buildings in the country. But adobes were not all the town was known for. The early people had discovered jade, a green stone worth a lot of money. They had learned how to cut the jade into beautiful forms, which made the stone worth even more. Because of this, tourists filled the town.

That was the trouble! Each tourist who came to the town was a new chance for Pedro to make up a new story. He wanted so much to be a person of mystery that he would say almost anything. He told stories that no one would believe.

Once he tried to make a tourist believe that a chunk of dirt was pure gold. The tourist took the chunk and made it crumble. "Gold doesn't crumble," the tourist said and walked away.

Pedro's parents began to worry.

"Your mother's worried about you," said Pedro's papa. "It is a mystery to us why you must tell stories."

"Mother's not worried about me," said Pedro.

Pedro's papa called out, "Marita, please come here." Pedro's mother came into the room.

"Pedro says you are not worried about these stories he tells," said Pedro's papa.

"I am worried," said Marita. "I worry about why he must try to make himself such a mystery. You are worth enough as you are, Pedro."

Pedro shrugged. "I like it when the tourists look at me curiously," he said.

"But the things you say are pure lies," said his father quietly.

"Papa, how is a lie different from a story?" Pedro wanted to know.

But his mother answered. "They are the same except for one thing," she said. "A story is told to make at least one person feel good. A lie always makes at least one person feel like a fool."

That afternoon, Pedro walked around his town. There were a great number of tourists. He tried hard to keep his mind off stories that he might tell them. When a woman asked him the time, he couldn't open his mouth.

"I didn't mean to startle you," she said.

"Oh, no, you didn't startle me," he said. "I don't know what time it is, though."

"Thank you anyway," the woman said.

"You see," Pedro continued. "I lost my watch. I put it in a small earthen jar outside my tent. It seemed secure. But during the night, a huge bear. . . ." He stopped, because the woman was looking at him with a curious gaze.

He thought, "Oh no, I'm doing it again." He began to run. He wanted to get as far from that woman as he could. He charged down the street. He ran forward, right through a group of people.

"Hey! Hold it! We're trying to make a movie here." Pedro looked around. Sure enough, he was right in the middle of a scene from a movie.

"I'm sorry," he said. He began to back up under an awning, where two people sat in the shade.

"Hey," the same man shouted. "Don't go under there. That awning is only for the stars."

He saw that the two people were stars. He remembered the man from movies he had seen. He knew that the man's name was Edward Bard.

"I'm sorry, Mr. Bard," he said to the man who was looking at Pedro curiously.

"That's all right," Mr. Bard said, smiling. "In fact, I'm glad you came by. Can you ride?"

"Oh, yes. I am a GOOD rider, Mr. Bard," said Pedro, who never rode anything. "I can ride almost any kind of animal."

"Can you ride a burro?" asked Mr. Bard.

"A burro?" Pedro repeated. He tried to look eager about the idea. "YOU are asking ME if I can ride a burro? Boys in this town grow up on burros. I am an expert," he said.

"Good," said Mr. Bard. "Would you like to be in this movie?"

"Oh, yes. Yes, I would!" said Pedro.

"Well, first go over to the brown trailer. Someone will give you a bundle of clothes to wear," said Mr. Bard. "Then go to the blue trailer. That is where they have make-up in little jars. Have them give you darker hair and browner skin."

As Pedro nodded, Mr. Bard continued, "Then go over to the red awning. The man under that awning is a special kind of artist. This artist is a little like a cartoonist. Like any cartoonist, he draws scenes inside little boxes and puts in words for what people say. The pictures made by the artist are the plan we follow when we make the movie. Ask him to show you the pictures for the boy with a burro. That is your part."

Pedro did as he was told. He was partly excited and partly very, very scared. Every eye seemed to gaze at him. He went to the tent for a special pair of pants and shirt. He went to the make-up trailer, where they covered his hair with dark cream from a jar. Then they covered his face and hands with another kind of cream. Finally, he went to the cartoonist. The large drawings this man made were called "storyboards," Pedro learned. He studied them carefully. The pictures showed Pedro just how he was supposed to ride the burro.

"There's the burro," said Mr. Bard. "Hop on."

Pedro had never seen a burro, except in books. He was glad to see that it was so small and dainty. "This shouldn't be hard," he thought.

A woman held the burro securely. She had a curious smile on her face. Pedro took a running start and jumped. For a minute, he had a secure seat on the burro. The next minute, however, the burro had shrugged him off. Pedro got up slowly. He tried to smile.

He stepped forward again. This time he laid across the burro's back. His plan was to throw one leg over and then sit up. The burro bowed its back legs, and Pedro was dropped to the ground again like a bundle of rags.

"Would you like some help?" the woman asked Pedro.

"Yes," Pedro said quietly. "I would like a little help. You see, I have never seen a burro just like this one before."

At last, Pedro got settled securely on the burro. He held onto its hair. The burro began to move down the street. Everyone was quiet.

Just then, the burro began to bray. It was the most terrible sound Pedro had ever heard in his life. "Hee-haw, hee-haw," the animal said. The way it brayed made it sound as if it were in pain.

"Keep your burro quiet!" shouted someone.

Pedro pulled on the hair of the burro's neck. To his horror, the braying got louder.

"Keep that animal quiet!" the person shouted.

Still, the burro just kept braying and walking in dainty steps down the street.

"Don't you know how to make a burro stop braying?" the person shouted angrily.

Pedro was no longer curious about movies. He didn't care anymore if they all knew he had lied.

Pedro shouted, "No, how do I make it stop?"

Suddenly all the faces around him began to crumble into smiles. "YOU TELL IT A STORY!" all the people shouted. Everyone began to laugh. Pedro turned bright red. They had known all along that he didn't know how to ride a burro.

"Mother's right," he said to himself. "Telling a lie always makes a fool out of someone."

THINK ABOUT IT

1. Why were Pedro's parents worried about him?
2. Why were there a lot of people visiting the town in which Pedro lived?
3. Why do you think that Pedro made up stories?
4. If tourists came to visit your town, what would they most likely be coming to see?
5. What would you have said to Pedro if you were his parent?
6. Tell about the action that might have taken place in the movie during Pedro's scene.

Find Your Way

In "The Story Teller," you read that Pedro's town was well-known for its green jade. Make believe that you are on a trip to Pedro's town to find a lost, green jade jar. How would a map help you find it?

A map in a story or an article helps you learn more about what you are reading. The map shows where the green jade jar was hidden. Symbols are used to stand for places that will help you discover the hiding place. You can find out what each symbol stands for by looking at the list at the bottom of the map. This list is called a "legend."

Now look at the right-hand part of the map. How do you know where north, south, east, and west are?

Look at the map as you answer these questions:

1. Suppose you found the map in the sand near a big rock. In which direction should you walk to reach the pueblo?

2. In which direction should you go next in order to find the jar?

Have a treasure hunt with your classmates. Your group will have three "treasures" to hide somewhere in your classroom, in the school building, or on the school grounds. Decide where you want each object hidden and then hide them.

Now draw a treasure map with your group. Think about symbols to use to mark the spots that lead to the three hiding places. Also make up a legend that explains those symbols.

Trade maps with another group. See who can find all three treasures first.

Train Ride to Freedom

"Will it work?" "Will I be able to escape?"
These thoughts went around and around in Fred
Bailey's mind.

Fred was a slave who lived in Maryland in
the year 1838. He had learned to read and write,
and he was a skilled worker. But he was still
a slave. How Fred longed to be free!

Now Fred was planning to run away. Slaves could find freedom in the northern states, if they could only get there. "And I'm going to get there!" Fred told himself.

Fred had laid careful plans. He had sailor clothes hidden in the room of a sailor friend named Benny. He also had a small bag hidden there with all his belongings in it. Best of all, Benny was giving him his seaman's papers.

Without a pass of some kind or papers showing that he was free, a black man could not travel alone on southern trains. Benny was a free black man, and his seaman's papers would take Fred anywhere.

At sunup one day, Fred hurried across the town to the house where Benny had a room. No words were spoken except in whispers, as Benny helped Fred get dressed as a sailor. Then he gave Fred his seaman's papers.

"Now," Fred whispered, "I'll walk to the railroad station. I don't want to be seen carrying my bag, so I don't want it until the very last minute. Get someone to bring it to me just as the train is ready to pull out. He mustn't be a minute too early or a minute too late. If the timing isn't just right, I risk getting captured. Do you understand?"

"You've got it worked out perfectly, Fred," Benny said. "Don't worry."

"Let's hope it does work," Fred said. "If I get away, I don't know how I'll ever pay you back for your help, Benny. But I'll send your papers back to you the first chance I get."

"If you don't, I won't worry," Benny said with a smile. "I'll just tell the skipper I lost my papers and ask him to get me another copy."

Fred said good-by to Benny. With a wave of his hand, he started toward the station. He could hardly keep from running. Several times, he had to make himself slow down.

The train for the North was already at the station when Fred arrived, wearing sailor clothes. The engine was puffing. That was good, but the next few minutes could prove risky.

"What if my bag doesn't get here?" Fred thought. "What if somebody sees me who knows I'm a slave?" Benny's seaman's papers would be of no help to Fred then.

The train whistle blew and the engine gave a big puff. "All aboard!" the brakeman called.

At that very second, a horse-drawn cab came to a stop at the station. The driver jumped down from his seat and came running with a bag in his hand. A big smile came over Fred's face. He snatched the bag from the cabman. Then he jumped onto the train just as it started to move.

Aboard the train, Fred settled himself in a seat. "That was close!" he sighed.

The conductor came and stood at Fred's side. "Where's your ticket, sailor?"

Fred did not show any sign of fear. "I wasn't able to buy a ticket in the station, sir," Fred said. "I just had time to get on the train. I have the money in my pocket. I'd like to buy my ticket now, a ticket to Philadelphia."

The conductor nodded. But as he handed Fred the ticket, he said, "Let me see your free papers."

Fred tried hard to keep calm. "I don't have any free papers," he said honestly. "But I have something that will take me around the world. I have something with the American eagle on it."

Proudly Fred pulled out Benny's seaman's papers. Unfolding them, he handed them to the conductor. He hoped the conductor would not be too interested in the description of Benny that was on the papers. Benny was short and very dark in color. Fred did not match that description. He was tall, and his skin color was light brown.

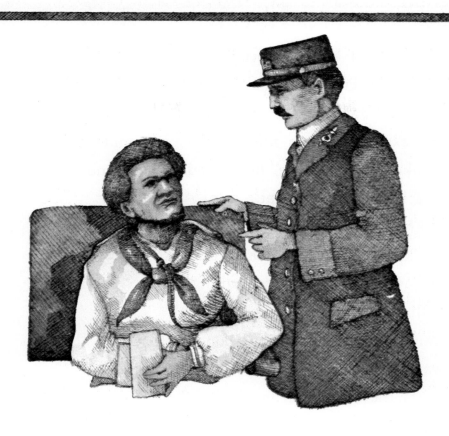

The conductor looked at the papers. Fred
held his breath. At last the conductor folded the
papers and handed them back to Fred.

That was not the last bad moment for the
runaway slave. At a certain stop, the train was
carried across the river by a ferryboat. Many
passengers left their seats during the ferry ride. It
was then that Fred came face to face with a
man he had worked for.

The man was looking straight at Fred. Their eyes met, and Fred saw the beginnings of a smile on the man's face. There was nothing he could do now except smile in return. The other man did not speak. After a while, he turned around and went back to his own seat.

"He knew me," Fred thought to himself. "I'm sure he knew me. He saw me running away from slavery, and he didn't say anything. I won't ever forget that good man."

Although there were many dangers for a runaway slave headed north, the most unsafe place was the city of Wilmington, Delaware. Wilmington was always full of slave-catchers watching for runaways. These men kept a very close eye on train stations and boat landings.

All railroad passengers going to Philadelphia had to change at Wilmington. They had to leave the train and take a boat the rest of the way. Fred was worried, fearing that he might be captured there.

However, Fred Bailey was lucky the day he went through Wilmington. None of the slave-catchers so much as looked his way.

Fred made the change to the boat along with the other passengers. No one who saw Fred suspected that he was a runaway.

Once on the boat, he began to feel safer. He thought about the beautiful name of Philadelphia, the city to which he was heading. He thought, too, about another name by which that city was sometimes known: "City of Brotherly Love." To Fred, Philadelphia was more like the "City of Freedom."

The big wheel of the boat splashed through the water. Suddenly, the city came into sight.

"This is free air I'm breathing," Fred thought as he stood on the deck. He was in sight of freedom! Suddenly, he felt like a king—like the ruler of the most wonderful land in the world!

From Philadelphia, Fred went on to New York. There, he married a free black woman. He and his wife went still farther north. In Massachusetts, Fred found a good job and friends and a real home at last.

But he could not use the name Fred Bailey anymore. It would not be wise. It might even lead to his capture and return to slavery.

Besides, a slave name did not seem to fit a free life. Why not leave the old name behind with the old life?

Fred heard these words from his friends and agreed with them. He decided to use the name Douglass. And as Frederick Douglass, he was to become famous.

Fred became a speaker, a writer of books, and editor of his own newspaper. For many years he was a leader in the fight against slavery. Crowds came to hear his speeches, and he often made his listeners want to work hard against slavery. Indeed, it was said that the powerful speeches of Frederick Douglass helped many slaves gain their freedom.

The man who had once been a slave came to be thought of as an important man of learning. The President of the United States asked him to serve the government. He sent Douglass to act as the American Minister to the country of Haiti.

Many years after his escape from slavery,
Frederick Douglass wrote a book about his life.
It is a moving and exciting book that you
may someday want to read.

THINK ABOUT IT

1. Why was Fred Bailey planning to run away?

2. Why did Fred need Benny's papers?

3. Why did Fred change his name?

4. For what did Frederick Douglass become famous?

5. While Fred was trying to make his escape, he ran into a man he had worked for. Did the man turn Fred in? Why or why not?

6. Do you think it was risky for a slave to run away? Why do you suppose so many slaves tried it?

7. In the days when there was slavery, it was against the law to try to help a runaway slave. Do you think this was a good law?

128

There Isn't Time

There isn't time, there isn't time
To do the things I want to do,
With all the mountain-tops to climb,
And all the woods to wander through,
And all the seas to sail upon,
And everywhere there is to go,
And all the people, every one
Who lives upon the earth, to know.
There's only time, there's only time
To know a few, and do a few,
And then sit down and make a rhyme
About the rest I want to do.

Eleanor Farjeon

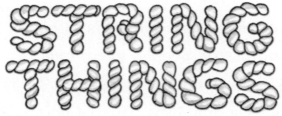

STRING THINGS

Would you like to make your room more interesting? Hanging things from the ceiling is one way to do that, and a String Thing is one decoration you can use. No one will be able to guess how it is made. Probably everyone will want you to explain it to them.

To make your String Thing, you will need some string, a balloon, a bowl of paste, a paper clip, and a rag. Be sure to read all of the directions before you begin to work. Your teacher will give you a special paste to use when you are ready to start.

1. Put your string into the bowl of paste, and leave it there until it becomes very wet.

2. Blow up your balloon fully and tie it.

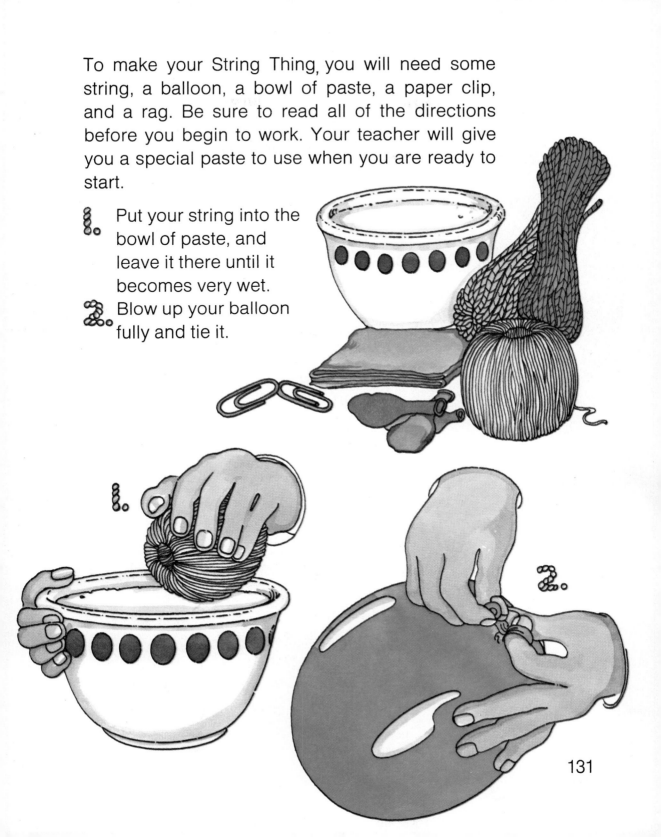

131

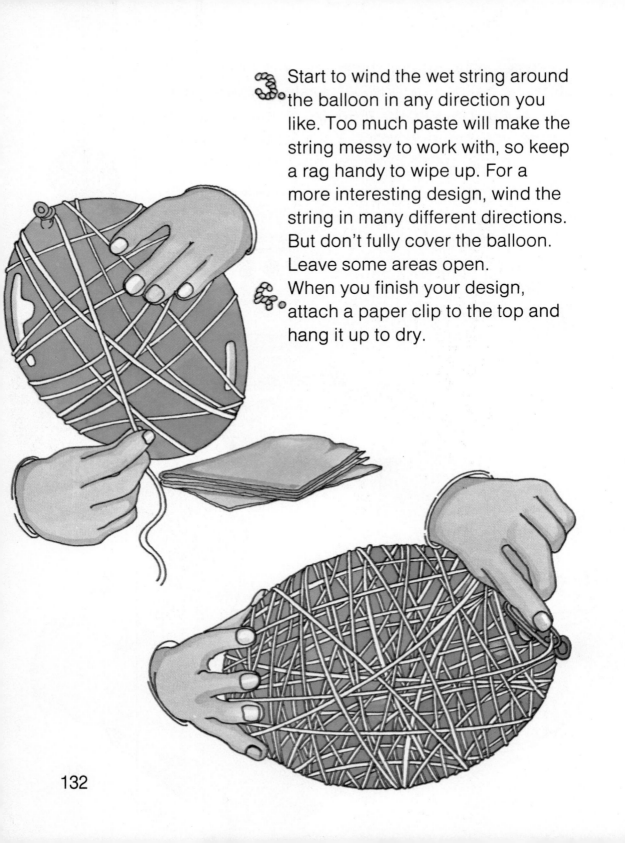

3. Start to wind the wet string around the balloon in any direction you like. Too much paste will make the string messy to work with, so keep a rag handy to wipe up. For a more interesting design, wind the string in many different directions. But don't fully cover the balloon. Leave some areas open.

When you finish your design, attach a paper clip to the top and hang it up to dry.

132

5. When the string dries, it will be stiff. Pop the balloon and remove it through one of the open areas.

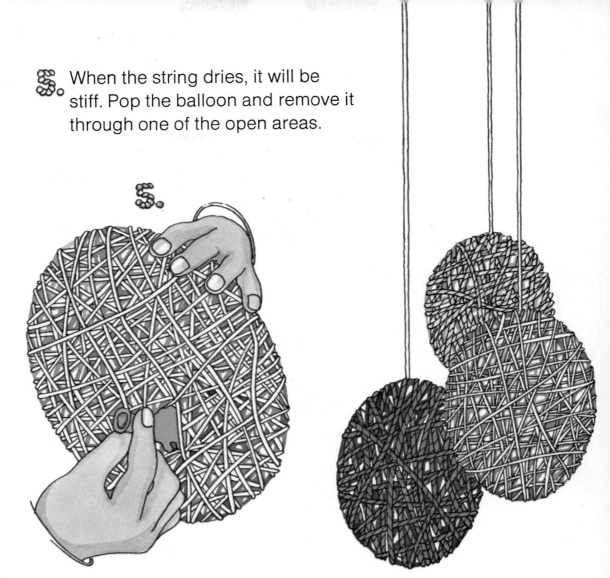

Your String Thing is now ready to hang. If you would like something more colorful, you can use colored yarn instead of string. You may want to make several String Things to decorate your room. If you are careful with them, they will probably last a long time.

The World's Best-Known Lamb

It was a cold morning in the spring of the year 1818. A girl named Mary Elizabeth Sawyer was helping her father with their farm animals. After feeding the cows, they went to the sheep pen. There they discovered that two lambs had been born during the night.

One of the new lambs was very weak, so Mary took the lamb into their house to care for it. First, she wrapped the little animal in some soft cloths. Then she sat down close to the fire with the lamb in her lap. All day and all night, Mary watched the lamb. Several times she tried to give it some tea or warm milk.

At first the lamb was too weak to drink, but toward evening, it took its first swallow of warm tea. During the night, it was able to drink a little more. By morning, the lamb was stronger. It was able to stand up for the first time. It was really hungry, too, and began to drink lots of milk.

"The lamb will be all right now," Mary thought. "There's no reason to worry anymore."

From that day on, the little lamb grew steadily stronger. Whenever Mary called, it came trotting to her side. It followed her around and lay down at her feet when she sat. The lamb wasn't just one of the farm animals. It had all the freedom of any well-loved pet.

One day Mary and her brother decided to take the lamb to school. Off they went with the lamb trotting along behind them. They reached the school ahead of their teacher and most of their schoolmates. Only a few friends saw them take the lamb into the schoolhouse.

Mary hid the lamb under her desk and covered it so that its white coat—called "fleece"—did not show. The lamb was so quiet that it might not have been discovered all day. However, during the morning, Mary was called on to recite, to tell what she knew about the lesson.

In those days, pupils had to stand at the front of the room when they recited. As soon as Mary left her desk, the lamb jumped up and trotted along after her.

There must have been a great deal of laughter in that schoolroom. Boys and girls stood up to see Mary and her lamb. They jumped up and down, pointing and waving and laughing.

Mary was the only person who didn't feel like laughing. She took the lamb outside to a shed and left it there until it was time to go home.

As one story goes, there was a visitor in school that day—a young man named John Roulstone. The very next day John Roulstone visited the school again. Walking straight to Mary's desk, he handed her a piece of paper. Here is what was written on it.

Mary had a little lamb,
    Its fleece was white as snow;
And everywhere that Mary went,
    The lamb was sure to go.

It followed her to school one day,
    Which was against the rule.
It made the children laugh and play
    To see a lamb in school.

The poem about Mary and her lamb became one of the best-known poems in the world. It made Mary and her pet famous, too. Today, you may visit the house in Sterling, Massachusetts, where Mary lived as a girl. You may also visit the little schoolhouse, which has been moved to Sudbury, Massachusetts.

Over the years, other funny poems have been written about Mary and her lamb. Have you ever heard any of these?

Mary had a little lamb,
   Its fleece as white as snow;
And everywhere that Mary went
   —She took a bus.

Mary had a little lamb,
   Its coat was white as cotton;
And everywhere that Mary went,
   That lamb came a-trottin'.

Mary had a little lamb,

    She set it on the shelf;

And every time it wagged its tail,

    It spanked its little self.

THINK ABOUT IT

1. How did it happen that Mary's lamb became a family pet?

2. One day, Mary took her lamb to school. Was the lamb discovered right away? When was it discovered?

3. How do you think Mary felt when her lamb was discovered?

4. Would you be surprised to see a lamb in school? Would you be surprised to see some other kind of pet? Why or why not?

Heat Wave

The city of Regalia lay baking in the summer sunshine like a pie. On the sidewalks, it was hot enough to fry an egg. In fact, many people fried their eggs on the sidewalks because it was too hot to work in their kitchens. At night hundreds and hundreds of people went to sleep in Middle Park because their homes were too hot. They covered the dry grass like fallen leaves. And every morning they looked damply at each other and said, "Hot enough for you?" But nobody laughed.

King Lester sat on his throne roasting in his purple robe. He looked out the window of the throne room, which was on the top floor of the tallest skyscraper in Regalia. From there he could see over the roofs to the ocean, which beat against the fringe of the city.

The beaches were covered with people trying to cool off. There were so many of them that there seemed to be one person to every dot of sand.

"Sir, it is so hot that no one can work," said Count Cambridge, who worked in the Royal Office. "This heat is getting serious."

"Send for Dr. Kermit and his Magic Spell Book," growled the King. "It is time he earned his pay."

In a very few moments a little, golden plane landed. Dr. Kermit got out. He came into the throne room carrying a thick black book.

"See if you can cool things off a bit," said the King. "And be quick about it."

Dr. Kermit opened his book of magic to page thirty and read out a Cold Spell. At once a block of solid ice formed around King Lester.

"That should do the trick," said Dr. Kermit.
He shut his Spell Book with a bang and left.

Count Cambridge tore his hair. Then he rushed
to the telephone and called Jimmy Fish the Fixer.

Jimmy was now a prince of Regalia. He was
married to the King's daughter. But he still fixed
things and thought up new things because that
was what he liked best to do.

He breezed over to the King's office in his fast
little car. He shot up to the throne room in the
elevator. When he saw what had happened, he
set to work.

"Open the windows," he ordered. He called six of the royal guards to help him. They all pushed the big block of ice over to the open windows where the sun could shine on it. In two minutes it had melted.

The first thing everyone heard as the ice cracked open was a roar from the King.

"Fire Dr. Kermit," he cried. When he had calmed down a bit, he said, "Jimmy, something must be done about this heat."

Jimmy shook his head sadly.

"I know, Your Majesty," he said. "I've been thinking about it for a long time. But I'm afraid even I can't think up a machine that will cool the whole city."

The King sighed and sat down to think. Jimmy sat down, too with his head in his hands.

Suddenly the whole skyscraper shook. The glass in the windows rattled.

"What now?" cried the King. Lifting his royal robe off the floor, he dashed outside with Jimmy close behind him.

On the hills behind the city stood a giant. He was so tall that the skyscrapers came up only to

the middle of his legs. He wore a long
swimsuit and a big straw hat. He took another
step toward Regalia, and the ground shook under
his feet.

"Oh, help," said the King in a weak voice. "As
if we didn't have enough trouble . . ."

The giant opened his mouth and a great and
terrible roar came out, louder than the loudest
thunder.

The King turned to Count Cambridge. "Call out
the army," he said.

But Jimmy held up a hand and said, "Wait. Let's not be too quick about this."

"Hello, down there," the giant roared. "Can you hear me?"

King Lester made a face. "He must be a fool! Hear him? My ears will never be the same again. Ask him what he wants."

"Good morning," Jimmy shouted. "I'm speaking for the great King Lester the Sixth. Please keep your voice down to a gentle whisper and tell us if you come in war or peace."

The giant took off his hat and mopped his face with a dirty cloth that was bigger than Middle Park. "Oh, I'm not looking for trouble," he said, speaking more quietly. "It's just so hot that I want to get into the water. You've got the best beach up around here. I was hoping you'd let me go in it where it's shallow. You see," he added, "I can't swim very well."

"I suppose if we don't let him, he'll stamp the city flat," said King Lester angrily. "But maybe we should call out the army and have him shot down."

"No, no, Your Majesty," said Jimmy. "If he fell, he'd smash us all. I have an idea. Tell everyone to clear the beaches and the streets."

The King didn't like it, but he trusted Jimmy. His order went out, and in a short time all the citizens of Regalia were safely in their houses. Then Jimmy shouted directions to the giant. The giant stepped right over the city and stood in the foam at the edge of the sea. He left his hat on the beach and walked into the water. Then, slowly, so as not to make a big wave, he let himself down into the water. His cheers and howls of joy cracked six hundred and fifty windows, but nothing else went wrong.

At last he crawled out and sat down on the beach. Jimmy called to him, "Now then, Giant, will you please fan yourself with your hat."

Glad to be helpful, the giant did so. The cool
wind from the great hat rushed through all the
streets of the city. It aired out rooms and
offices. It blew through the park. It cooled the
sidewalks.

King Lester leaned back. He opened his royal
robe with a happy smile. "The perfect answer to
a heat wave," he said. "A hat wave."

1. What was the weather like in Regalia at the time of the story?

2. What did Dr. Kermit do to try to make King Lester more comfortable? Did it work?

3. Why had the giant come to Regalia?

4. What did Jimmy Fish the Fixer ask the giant to do with his hat? How did this change the weather in Regalia?

5. Which part of the story did you think was the funniest?

6. Think of another way to make it cooler in Regalia. Your answer can be silly or serious.

7. What do you do to keep cool when the weather is very hot?

four

Laughing Time

It was laughing time, and the tall giraffe
Lifted his head and began to laugh:

Ha! Ha!   Ha! Ha!

And the chimpanzee on the ginkgo tree
Swung merrily down with a tee-hee hee:

Hee! Hee!   Hee! Hee!

"It's certainly not against the law!"
Croaked old black crow with a loud guffaw:

Haw! Haw!   Haw! Haw!

The dancing bear who could never say ''No''
Waltzed up and down on the tip of his toe:

Ho! Ho!   Ho! Ho!

The donkey daintily took his paw,
And around they went: Hee-Haw! Hee-Haw!

Hee-Haw!   Hee-Haw!

The moon had to smile as it started to climb;
All over the world it was laughing time!

Ho! Ho!   Ho! Ho!   Hee-Haw!   Hee-Haw!
Hee! Hee!   Hee! Hee!   Ha! Ha!   Ha! Ha!

William Jay Smith

153

MASKS

Masks have been worn for many years by people all over the world. In some places, masks were believed to be magic. They were worn in dances asking for rain to help the corn grow. In Japan, actors sometimes wore masks to help them look like the characters they were playing. Today masks are most often worn for fun.

Masks can be any size or shape. They can be the faces of animals, things, or people. Masks can be made from wood, paper, metal, or even stone.

You can make a mask that will look like metal from heavy silver foil. You'll need a sheet of silver foil, white glue, scissors, and cardboard. If you want to decorate your mask, you can use buttons, yarn, string, colored construction paper, or beads. Read all of this article carefully. Then gather your supplies before you begin to work.

First, decide what kind of mask you want to make. Then cut a shape from the foil to make the main part of the mask.

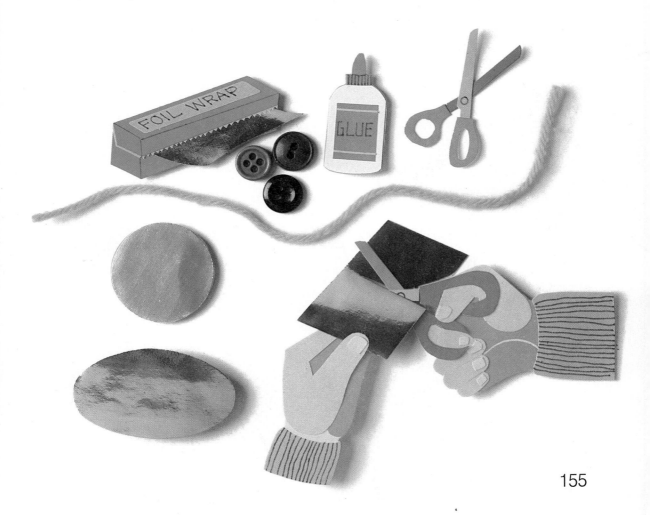

You can cut out a nose, ears, eyelids, and so on, from your leftover foil. Leave a tab on each part for gluing to the mask. Squirt a little white glue on the tab and on the mask, wait a few minutes, and then press them together. If you like, you can use construction paper instead of silver foil for these parts. Glue them to the mask the same way you would if you were using foil.

Pieces of yarn or string can be used for hair. Squirt glue on one end of each piece and press them to the mask. You can also make hair from strips of curled silver foil. Curl the foil by wrapping the strips around a pencil. Experiment to see how tight a curl you like. Then glue the best ones to your mask.

If you are going to wear your mask, cut out holes for the eyes and mouth. If you want to use it as a wall decoration, you can glue on eyes and a mouth. Buttons or beads can be used. You can even crumple pieces of foil into interesting shapes and use them. Try using the foil with the wrong side showing for a different look.

Cardboard glued to the back of the mask will give it enough strength to hang. Make a small hole at the top for hanging. Your mask is now ready to dress up a room or to dress up you!

Word of Mouth

Strawberry shortcake! Blueberry pie!
V-I-C-T-O-R-Y!
That's the way to spell it.
Here's the way to yell it: VICTORY!

This school cheer is known to many children who have never met each other and who have never read the cheer in a book. Yet, somehow, the rhyme got around. So have countless other rhymes, cheers, songs, and stories. Boys and girls make them up and use them. Other children hear them and repeat them. Passing things on in this way is called "word of mouth."

There was a time when almost all information was passed by word of mouth. Town criers had the job of going through a town calling out important news for all to hear. Travelers also repeated news as they went from place to place. News was often put in the form of songs and stories as it traveled.

These days, we get our information from books, magazines, and newspapers. Radio, TV, and movies are also sources of information. All these different sources have replaced the old word-of-mouth way.

Or have they?

There is one group of people who are still passing on songs, stories, and games by word of mouth. This group is *you*—schoolchildren. On countless playgrounds and streets, you can hear children singing the same songs and telling the same riddles and rhymes.

A pointless rhyme that countless children have fun with is:

What's your name?
Puddin' Tame. Ask me again,
And I'll tell you the same!

Have you ever jumped rope or played ball to this rhyme?

> **A—my name is *Alice*.**
> **My friend's name is *Archie*.**
> **We come from *Alaska*.**
> **And we sell *apples*.**

From A to Z, the player must add words that name two persons, a place, and a thing—all beginning with the same letter.

Here is another ageless rhyme that is used to choose who goes first in a game.

> **One potato, two potato,**
> **Three potato, four;**
> **Five potato, six potato,**
> **Seven potato, more;**
> **And out goes *Y-O-U*!**

Have you ever told a pointless story just for fun? Chances are that some of the nonsense stories you tell are ageless. Here is a piece of nonsense that your grandparents may have known—or even your great-grandparents.

Ladles and jelly spoons,
I stand upon this speech to make a platform.
The train arrived in—has not yet come,
So I took a bus and walked.
Now I come before you to stand behind you
And tell you something I know nothing about!

Why are the same riddles, songs, and nonsense rhymes known around the world? Perhaps it's because children—no matter where they live or what language they speak—are much the same. They like to laugh at the same kinds of things and pass them on by word of mouth.

THINK ABOUT IT

1. What does it mean to say that something is passed on by "word of mouth"?

2. How did people who lived long ago get the news?

3. Today, how do we get our information?

4. What is still passed on by word of mouth today?

5. What do you think often happens to a story that is passed on by word of mouth?

6. Do you think that children who live years from now will know the same rhymes and songs that you know?

7. Which do you think is the better way to get important news—by word of mouth or from TV? Why?

163

The One in the Middle Is the
Green Kangaroo

Freddy Dissel had two problems. One was his older brother, Mike. The other was his younger sister, Ellen. Freddy thought a lot about being the one in the middle. He felt squeezed between Mike and Ellen.

Every year Mike got new clothes. Freddy didn't because Mike's old clothes fit him just fine.

Freddy used to have a room of his own. But when Ellen was born, Freddy moved in with Mike. Now Ellen had a room of *her* own.

Freddy imagined things would never get better for him. He would always be a great big middle nothing!

Then Freddy Dissel heard about the school play. Mike had never been in a play. Ellen had never been in a play. This was his chance to be special. Freddy decided he would try it.

He waited two whole days before he went to his teacher. "Ms. Gumber," he said, "I want to be in the school play."

Ms. Gumber smiled and shook her head. "I'm sorry, Freddy," she said. "The play is being done by the big boys and girls like Mike."

Freddy looked at the floor and sighed. He started to walk away.

"Wait a minute, Freddy," Ms. Gumber called. "I'll talk to Ms. Matson. She's in charge of the play. Maybe they need some help."

Later, Ms. Gumber told Freddy to go to the auditorium. When he got there, Ms. Matson was waiting for him. Freddy walked up to her and said, "I want to be in the play." Ms. Matson asked him to go up on the stage and say that again in a very loud voice.

Freddy looked out at Ms. Matson from the stage. "I AM FREDDY," he shouted. "I WANT TO BE IN THE PLAY."

"Good," Ms. Matson called. "Now then, Freddy, can you jump?"

What kind of question was that, Freddy wondered. Of course he could jump. So he did. He jumped all around the stage. When he was through, Ms. Matson clapped her hands and said,

"I think you will be fine as the Green Kangaroo, Freddy. It's a very important part."

Freddy didn't tell anyone at home about the play until dinner time. Then Freddy said, "Guess what, everyone. I'm going to be in a play. I'm going to be the Green Kangaroo!"

Mike was so surprised that he knocked over a whole glass of milk. Ellen laughed because Mike spilled his milk. While Mike cleaned up, Freddy just sat there and smiled.

"What did you say?" Mike asked.

"I said I'm going to be the Green Kangaroo in the school play!" Freddy answered.

"That sounds wonderful," his dad said with a big smile.

His mom kissed him right at the dinner table. "We're all proud of you," she said.

For the next two weeks Freddy had to practice being the Green Kangaroo. He practiced at school and at home. He made kangaroo faces in the mirror and did kangaroo jumps on his bed. He even dreamed about kangaroos.

Finally the day of the play came. Freddy was up at dawn, practicing. The whole family and many neighbors planned to be there.

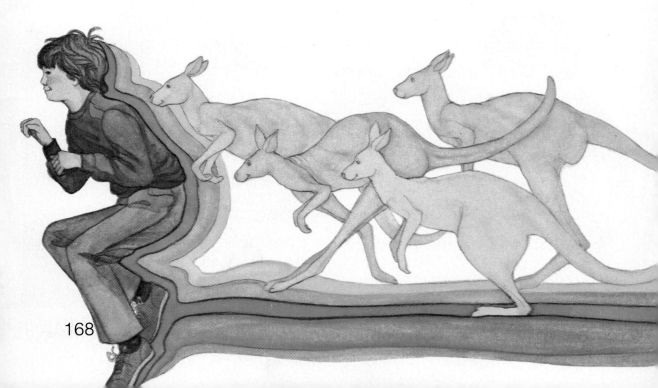

After lunch Ms. Gumber called to Freddy, "Time to go now. Time to get into your suit."

Freddy went to Ms. Matson's room. She helped Freddy into his Green Kangaroo suit, which covered all of him. It even had green feet. Only his face stuck out. Ms. Matson put some green dots on it.

Soon it was time for the play to begin. Freddy waited backstage with the older boys and girls. He tried to smile at them but the smile wouldn't come. His heart started to beat faster. He felt funny. Then Ms. Matson said, "They're waiting for for you, Freddy. Go ahead."

He jumped out onto the stage and looked into the audience. It was very quiet. He could hear his heart. He thought he saw his mom and dad and Ellen. He thought he saw Mike and his own class and Ms. Gumber and all of the neighbors, too. They were all out there in the middle of the audience. But for once Freddy wasn't in the middle. He was all by himself up on the stage.

Freddy smiled. His heart slowed down. He felt better. He smiled a bigger, wider smile.

"HELLO, EVERYONE," Freddy said. "I AM THE GREEN KANGAROO. WELCOME."

The play began. Every now and then one of the characters said to him, "And who are you?"

Freddy jumped around and answered, "Me? I am the Green Kangaroo!" It was fun. Every time he said it the audience laughed. Freddy liked it when they laughed.

When it was all over, everyone on the stage took a bow. Then Ms. Matson came out and said, "A special thank-you to Freddy Dissel. He played the part of the Green Kangaroo."

Freddy jumped over to the middle of the stage. He took a big, low bow all by himself. The audience clapped hard for a long time.

Freddy didn't care much about wearing Mike's clothes any more. He didn't care much about sharing Mike's room, either. He didn't even care much about being the one in the middle. He felt just great being Freddy Dissel.

THINK ABOUT IT

1. Why was Freddy so eager to be in the school play?

2. What part did Freddy get? What did he have to do to play his part?

3. How did Freddy feel when it came time to go out onto the stage? How did he feel after the play was over?

4. Have you ever been in a play? How did you feel when it was time to go out onto the stage? How did you feel when the play was over?

5. How do you think it would feel to be "the one in the middle," the oldest, the youngest, or the only child in your family?

DANGER!

Liz Baker ran lightly through the grass and down toward the pond. She went there every day after school to play with Nitwit. For Liz, these hours with her colt were always the best hours of the day.

Liz slowed down and then stopped. Something was wrong. The colt always watched for her, but today Nitwit was nowhere in sight.

"Nitwit!" Liz called. She could see her breath in the frosty air. "Nitwit, where are you?"

Nitwit answered her with a frightened whinny. When Liz heard it, her heart began to pound. The whinny had come from the swamp.

"Nitwit!" Liz cried out. "Nitwit!" She started to run toward the swamp at full speed.

Soon Liz spotted Nitwit through the tall grass. As she dashed toward the colt, she came to a barbed-wire fence, put up to keep Nitwit away from the swamp. Duchess, Nitwit's mother, had never needed a fence. She knew how to pick her way through the swamp with special care. But Nitwit hadn't learned that lesson yet. Liz saw that a fallen tree branch had pushed one of the fence posts to the ground. Nitwit had been able to step right over the barbed wire.

"If only Duchess had been here," Liz said to herself. "She would have watched her colt and kept him out of the swamp."

At last Liz reached the edge of the swamp, soft and spongy under a thin coating of ice. She heard the colt whinny.

"I'll get you out, Nitwit," she called. But her heart was filled with sadness. She thought of her plans to train the colt and someday to ride him. Liz knew the dangers of the swamp with its many mud-filled holes. If Nitwit stepped into one of them, his young legs would go down quickly. He might even break a leg, trying to get free. And if that happened. . . . Liz set her lips. She didn't really want to think about that.

Liz took a careful step. The frosty ground seemed solid. But when she let her whole weight down on one foot, her leg sank into mud up to the knee.

"I'll have to go for help," Liz thought as she slowly lifted her leg from the mud. She didn't want to leave Nitwit. She could see the colt shaking with fear, but getting help was the only way to save him. As fast as she could, Liz ran back toward her house.

When she reached the farmhouse, she was out of breath. "Mom! Nitwit's stuck in the swamp! I need your help to get him out."

"Liz!" her mother said, frowning when she saw the muddy leg of her pants. "You didn't go in after him, did you?"

"No, Mom. Just one step. I knew it would be silly to go in farther."

Mrs. Baker reached for her jacket. "Your father's in the west field. We'll pick him up in the truck and then go straight to the swamp. We need all the help we can get."

"Please may I go back to the swamp now?" Liz pleaded. "I want to be near Nitwit until you and Dad come. Maybe if I talk to him, I can keep him calm so that he won't hurt himself!"

Mrs. Baker nodded. "That silly colt has no sense!" she declared. "Now I see why you call him Nitwit! Hurry!" she added. "Get some rope from the barn before you go."

Liz raced to the barn as her mother left in the truck. She couldn't waste a minute. Maybe even now they were too late.

Duchess was standing quietly in the barn. As Liz grabbed for the rope, the mare whinnied hello.

"Your colt's in the swamp! Couldn't you have put some sense into his head?" Liz cried. "It's all your fault!"

But Liz knew that she was being unfair. "Duchess!" she cried out. "You know the swamp! You've been in and out a hundred times. Dad told me himself that he feels safe in the swamp if you're with him. You're the one to help me save Nitwit!"

She led Duchess out of the barn to the fence. Then she climbed the fence and slid over onto Duchess's back, gripping it tightly with her knees. "Here we come, Nitwit!" she yelled.

Not even a racehorse could have moved fast enough for Liz. She hurried Duchess and told her of the danger that Nitwit faced. It seemed to take forever to reach the swamp.

"Nitwit!" Liz called as loudly as she could. "Nitwit!"

When the colt's whinny came back to them, Duchess's ears went up sharply. She heard the cry of her colt and sensed that he was in some kind of trouble.

Then Duchess started into the swamp. Liz loosened her grip on the reins and watched as the mare picked her way through the spongy swampland. Duchess knew where it was safe to walk and where danger lay.

Liz closed her eyes tightly and wished hard. "Please let Nitwit be all right! Please let us be able to pull him out!"

The colt's whinny was suddenly close, and Liz opened her eyes as Duchess came to a stop. Liz stared. Nitwit's back was just about covered with mud. The colt was stuck fast!

"Take it easy, Nitwit," Liz said softly, trying to keep the fear out of her voice. "We'll get you out of there."

Liz looped one end of the rope, took careful aim, and tossed the loop around the colt's neck. Then she fastened the other end of the rope around Duchess's neck.

"The rest is up to you. Back, Duchess, back!" Liz yelled, pulling the reins.

Duchess backed up, step by step, and Nitwit was slowly pulled from the mud. Once he seemed about to slip back in again. Duchess leaned on the rope and whinnied sharply to the colt. He seemed to understand and to try a little harder. At last he found footing on solid ground.

"You're free!" Liz cried, her voice singing with gladness. She slid to the ground and hugged the muddy, shivering colt. "It's all right now." Then she turned to Duchess and hugged her, too. "You were wonderful, Duchess!"

Liz left the rope on the horses and walked beside the colt. Duchess led them safely out of the swamp just as her parents drove up in the truck.

179

"Is everything all right?" called Mrs. Baker.

Liz nodded. "Duchess took care of it all."

Mr. Baker smiled. "It's good that you thought of Duchess and didn't go into that swamp alone. I would have had to go back for her myself, and that would have wasted time. It might have been too late for Nitwit."

Liz gave Duchess a friendly pat and turned to the colt. "I don't know how such a smart mother could have such a silly colt," she said. "But I guess you've learned a lesson today."

Nitwit threw back his head and whinnied.

THINK ABOUT IT

1. At the beginning of the story, how did Liz know that her colt was in danger?

2. What did Duchess know how to do that Nitwit had not yet learned?

3. How did Liz get Nitwit out of the swamp?

4. How would Liz's father have removed Nitwit?

5. Do you think Liz planned all along to try to rescue Nitwit herself?

6. What would you have done if you had been Liz?

ONE FOR THE
COMPUTO

It all started because of Albert Einstein Smedley. I found this big old box we wanted to put up into the tree in my backyard. It was going to make a great tree house. Then Albert, who's a brain, poked his nose into our plan. One thing led to another. First thing you know, we're not building a tree house. We're building something called a "Computo."

My friends and I were thinking about how to get the box up into the tree when along came old Albert.

"Thomas!" Albert said to me. "What are you going to do with that box? Do you have an idea in mind?"

Albert never had just a simple plan for doing things. It had to be a well-thought-out idea. His parents are always bragging about how Albert is going to be a great scientist someday. Well, we didn't want any big brains like Albert hanging around, so I said, "Well, I guess that's one for our Computo to answer."

"Computo?" Albert said. "You must mean *computer*. But it's too involved, too technical, for someone who is not a scientist to make a computer out of an old box!"

"You mean you've never heard of a Computo?" Ray said, poking me. "It's a lot like a computer. You just feed a question into it. Then it whirs, and little lights blink. After a while, out pops the answer."

"It's not 'too technical' to make a Computo if you know about machines," I said. "We do. We're good mechanics."

Albert's face was very red. He said, "I have a fine lab at home. It's too technical to explain to you, but even with my lab I cannot make a machine that does what a computer does."

"You scientists don't know *everything*, Albert," Jane said

"Sure!" Bill added. "You need more than a science lab to build a Computo. We mechanics can do it because we have the know-how."

So that's how we got started building a Computo instead of a tree house. As it turned out, it wasn't such a bad idea after all.

The next morning we were working very hard in my backyard when Albert came along. He wanted to stay and learn how to build a Computo. So we let him.

We worked on the Computo all day. Mr. Duncan, our neighbor, who is a very good mechanic, helped us. He fixed all the lights in the Computo. We got an old sweeper and a beat-up fan and an old dog clipper. Mr. Duncan tested the Computo to make sure no one would get hurt.

We painted the Computo a great shade of green. Then we moved it into our front yard. After a while Mom got home from her job. Soon some other people dropped by to visit. One of them was Albert Smedley's mother.

Mom was curious about our invention as soon as she spotted it. "What kind of machine is that?" she asked.

"Please read the sign," I said.

"I give up!" Mom said. "How does it work?"

"If you wish to test the Computo," I said, "write something on this piece of paper. Then slip it in here with a nickel."

So Mom put her question in the Computo. All the little lights began to wink and blink. The sweeper ran. The fan turned. The dog clipper whirred. Everything made a terrible noise.

After a while the noise slowed down, and a slot opened. Out came the answer.

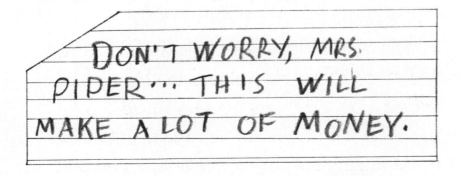

Mom laughed. "Well, well! That's something! Would anyone else care to try the Computo?"

"It's not a bad toy," Mrs. Smedley said. "However, Albert would be bored with it. He wouldn't get involved in such an idea."

"I'll ask it something," Annabelle's mother said. She found a nickel and wrote, "Who will help with the dishes tonight—Annabelle or her brother?"

This one made the Computo work hard, but the answer was good, very good.

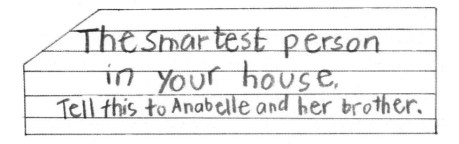

The smartest person in your house. Tell this to Anabelle and her brother.

"I'll tell them, Computo," Annabelle's mother said, laughing.

That was just the beginning of the Computo. The Dad's Club Carnival was the next night, and Mr. Duncan came up with the idea of taking our invention to the carnival. "You can make some money for a tree house," he said.

"A great idea," I said.

Well, the Computo was very busy at the carnival. After a while Mrs. Smedley came along. "Where in the world is Albert?" she said. "I haven't seen him since I got here."

Just then Mr. Duncan came by. "Hello there, Mrs. Smedley," he said smiling. "What do you think of the Computo?"

"It's all right for children," she said.

Mr. Duncan laughed. "Come on, now. It's a lot of fun. You ask Albert."

Mrs. Smedley kind of sniffed. "Albert is not interested in this child's toy. He's going to be a great scientist," she said.

"What has he made?" Mr. Duncan said.

"Why, nothing—yet. He's learning."

"Then," Mr. Duncan said, "you'll be proud to know he helped make the Computo work."

"I don't believe it!" she said.

Mr. Duncan winked at me. "Thomas," he said. "Ask the Computo where Albert is."

So I wrote, "Where is Albert?"

The Computo almost popped. It shivered and shook, and after a while the answer came out of the slot.

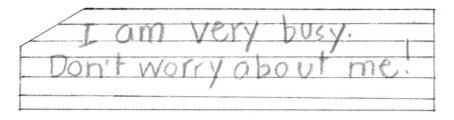

I am very busy.
Don't worry about me!

Mrs. Smedley turned red. "Is Albert in that—that thing?" she asked.

"He sure is!" Mr. Duncan said. "Albert is busy writing up these answers. He's not bored at all!"

"That's right, Mrs. Smedley," I said. "Soon it will be Albert's turn to run the sweeper and the fan and the clipper."

Mrs. Smedley stood and watched the Computo for a long time. It was very busy. At last Mrs. Smedley said, "Thomas, please give me a piece of paper."

She wrote a question. "Would the Computo like a hamburger?"

The Computo shook. The lights blinked. The answer came out.

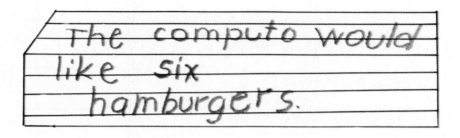

The computo would like six hamburgers.

The hamburgers were very good. Mrs. Smedley did not have to ask the Computo how many sodas to order.

1. At the beginning of the story, what were the children planning to do with the box?

2. How did it happen that they decided to build a Computo instead?

3. What did the Computo do?

4. How did the Computo work?

5. Why didn't Mrs. Smedley think that her son Albert would be interested in the Computo?

6. Was Mrs. Smedley right about her son?

7. If you were Albert, would you have helped with the Computo? Why or why not?

FOLLOW ALONG

In "One for the Computo," Albert told his friends that computers are very involved, technical machines. He was right. Computers can do many different things with numbers and do them all with amazing speed.

If you watch a computer in action, it may look as if the computer can do everything. But a computer cannot think for itself the way a person can. In fact, a computer can't do *anything* until someone tells it what to do!

Have you ever wondered how a computer works? The diagram below shows the way in which computers operate. A diagram is a special kind of picture that helps explain what you see or

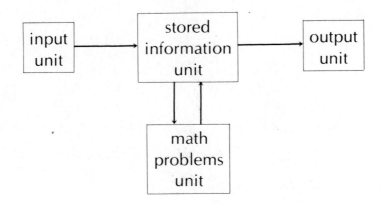

read. As you read more about computers below, use the diagram to help you understand what you are reading.

The first thing a computer needs is directions and information from the person operating it. This is called input. Find the input unit on the diagram.

All input is stored in another unit of the computer. The computer operator can retrieve any piece of information in that unit by telling the computer to recall it. Where is the stored information unit shown on the diagram?

Once all the needed input is stored, the operator can tell the computer to follow directions and recall information to do a math problem. The computer does this work in its math problems unit. Find it on the diagram.

The computer works in its own number language. The output unit changes the computer's answer into a language the operator can understand. Where is the output unit shown on the diagram?

Find a diagram in a book you use for school. Study it closely. Then write a paragraph about what the diagram tells you.

five

The Tale of the
Lazy Donkey

Paco and Rosita were donkeys that lived on a farm. Every day when Juan, their master, put the rope on Paco, he would say, "Paco, you are not like your sister, Rosita. What is wrong with you? Why are you so troublesome?"

In the morning while Juan was getting Paco ready to go into the fields, Paco would nibble on Juan's ear. Juan would push him away and say, "What's wrong, donkey?" This made Paco feel sad and very lonesome.

Sometimes, when Paco got tired, he would stop and rest. Again Juan would shout, "What's wrong, donkey?"

One sunny day, Paco stopped under the shade of a berry tree and began to nibble the berries. When Juan saw him, he roared, "I know what's wrong! You're just a lazy donkey!"

So that's what's wrong! thought Paco. Deep inside, Paco hurt. He wished he were like his sister. Rosita never wanted to play or eat berries in the shade on a hot day. She never got tired. Paco could not understand it. He was a very unhappy and lonesome donkey.

On the hottest day of the year, Paco just gave up. When Juan began to put him in harness, Paco would not let him. "Lazy donkey!" Juan shouted angrily.

Paco yawned and swished his tail. What more could a lazy donkey do? From that time on, Paco thought, "What's the use? I'm just troublesome."

Soon after that, on a market day, Juan harnessed Rosita to the cart. Then he shouted at Paco, "It's market day, and you, you lazy donkey, can't go!" Paco watched as Rosita and Juan went down the road. He could hear his master shouting, "Oh! That Paco! What a lazy donkey!" It made Paco very unhappy to hear Juan shout that way.

Another market day, after Juan had harnessed Rosita, he came back to see Paco. Juan was smiling. In fact, Paco had never seen him so happy. "Come, Paco. See what I have in the cart," said Juan in an excited voice.

There was a big pail of berries in the cart. Paco did not stop to think. He stuck his head in the pail and began to eat. This was food for a donkey king! While Paco nibbled the berries, Juan pushed him into the cart.

Paco blinked. Juan laughed a fearsome laugh. Then he shouted into Paco's ear, "You are going to market today, lazy donkey! Your sister will take you to market, and I will sell you for a handful of *pesos*!" Then Juan took away the pail of berries.

Paco blinked again with surprise. Juan had played a terrible trick on him. Paco would be truly lonesome without Rosita, but it would be good not to have this man shouting in his ears anymore. Paco yawned and swished his tail. Juan jumped into the cart, and they were off to the market in the city.

As the cart pulled onto the big wide road, all the cars slowed down. The people inside stretched their necks to look at the donkey being pulled by another donkey. Then they laughed.

Other donkeys pulling carts sneered when they saw Paco. An old, old donkey jeered, "Look at lazy Paco! He's so lazy his sister has to pull him in a cart!" How they all laughed!

After a while, Paco began to feel funny. He had never felt this way before. He wanted to hide his head. He closed his eyes tightly and tried not to listen, but the laughter grew louder and louder. Paco felt ashamed. Was he really so troublesome?

When they reached the market at last, Juan began to shout, "Donkey! Donkey! Who will buy my donkey?"

Many people came to the cart. Someone shouted, "That donkey is too lazy to walk to the market by himself!"

Juan said, "Yes. He is truly a lazy donkey. But he will keep your grass short." The people laughed and the donkeys brayed. How unhappy and ashamed Paco felt!

Again Juan shouted, "One *peso* and he's yours! Who will buy this donkey?"

A little man hopped up on the cart and handed Juan a *peso.* "He looks like a good donkey. I will take him." Again the people laughed and the donkeys brayed.

"Hello, Paco. I am Carlos. I do not care if the people laugh. We are going to be friends." Carlos put his hand on the donkey's neck and led him off the cart. Carlos was a kind man, Paco knew. He did not have Juan's fearsome smile.

Paco was glad to go with Carlos. Everyone at the market was laughing at him because he was so lazy. Paco walked with his head low. He was very ashamed.

Another donkey with a cart waited under a tree. "This is José," said Carlos. "José, this is Paco, our new friend. He is going to live with us. He'll work with us, too. Because there are now two *good* donkeys, there will be only half as much work to do."

All along the road leading out of the city, Carlos said, "What a *good* donkey, Paco. *Good* donkey!" Little by little, Paco began to lift up his head. Something new was happening. By the time they reached Paco's new home, Paco's head was high. He belonged to a man who thought he was really good! Well, he would try to be good.

The next morning, Carlos led Paco to the cart. Without thinking, Paco nibbled Carlos's ear. But Carlos did not push Paco away as Juan had always done. Carlos smiled! "I like you, too," he said. As he harnessed Paco, Carlos said, "How lucky I am to have two good donkeys now. Today you work, Paco. Tomorrow you will rest, and José will work."

Paco wanted so much to please Carlos. As Paco pulled out onto the road, he heard another donkey say, "Can that be the same lazy Paco doing the work of a donkey?"

Paco brayed loud and clear, "Can't you see that I am not the same? I am no longer the lazy donkey of Juan. I am the *good* donkey of Carlos!"

Paco held his head high and opened his eyes wide to see better the big, wide road to the city.

THINK ABOUT IT

1. At the beginning of the story, Paco felt unhappy and lonesome. Why?

2. How did Juan trick Paco into getting into the cart?

3. What did Juan do with Paco?

4. Did Carlos act the same way toward Paco as Juan had acted? Explain your answer.

5. How did the way Carlos acted toward Paco change Paco?

6. If Juan had been nicer to Paco, do you think that Paco would have worked harder for him?

7. What lesson can you learn from this story?

Bread Clay

Many hundreds of years ago, bread was not used only for food. On special occasions, bakers molded bread either by hand or in molds to make unique decorations. There were even judges to decide who could make the fanciest breads.

But there was always the chance that baked bread decorations would be eaten! So someone made a bread clay to be used only for decorations. It looked like bread, but it hardened, and it could not be eaten.

You can use bread clay to make your own decorations. The next pages describe how to make the bread clay and how to mold it. Remember, do not try to eat it!

Before you begin to work, cover your desk top with a piece of wax paper. Tape it down so it won't move.

Your teacher will give you the materials needed to make the clay. Put everything in a bowl and mix it together with your hands until it is no longer sticky. Two people can do this together. When the clay is ready, tear it in half—one half for each of you.

There are many ways to work the clay. You can mold it, roll it, or cut it. When you work bread clay, use the same motions you would if you were working with play clay.

To form a ball, pull off a piece of clay and roll it around in the palms of your hands. A long roll can be made from a ball. Put the ball on the desk and roll it out with your fingers.

You can make a flat sheet of bread clay by rolling it out with a rolling pin. Any shape can be cut out with a sharp pencil point.

If you want to make your object permanent, you must brush it with a sealing mixture when it is finished. This can be made by mixing 2 tablespoons of white glue with 2 tablespoons of water. Be sure to cover the whole piece of clay with the mixture. Then allow your object to dry for 24 hours.

You can decorate bread clay after it dries. Try gluing on beads, feathers, or ribbon. You can also paint bread clay.

Bread clay objects make unique gifts that anyone would enjoy receiving. You might want to make several to keep on hand for special occasions.

The Fastest Car in the World

Freelan O. and Francis E. Stanley were twin brothers. They looked alike, dressed alike, and talked alike. The subject they liked to talk about most was inventions.

When people wanted to go somewhere in the late 1800's, they walked, rode a bicycle, or drove a horse and buggy. F.O. and F.E. had long talks about how they could invent a buggy that would go faster than one pulled by a horse.

During one of these talks, F.O. pulled at his long black beard and said to F.E., "Steam engines move trains. Steam engines move ships. Let's put a steam engine inside our buggy."

"Good idea," said F.E. "Steam will give us a lot of power. We ought to be able to build the fastest buggy in the world!"

They bought a steam engine and a boiler that had been built for use in a steamship. "If we use those big things," F.E. said, "our buggy will look like a mouse trying to carry a fat pig. Everyone will laugh at us!"

They went back to the builders and asked for a small engine and a small boiler. "It can't be done," the builders said. "If we substituted a smaller engine, it would fall apart the first time you tried it. This is the only size we can make. Sorry!"

"Well, let's try them anyway," said F.E.

The engine and the boiler didn't fit right or look right anywhere. Somehow the twins found a way to put them both under the floorboards. With all that added weight, the buggy looked as if it would fall apart any minute.

At last the buggy was finished. When the boiler was hot enough to make steam, F.O. and F.E. climbed into their seats. F.E. pushed up the throttle very slowly, and the buggy began to move. Down the street they went, with the buggy billowing steam and whistling very loudly.

"We're making more noise than a factory whistle at noon," said F.O. happily. "Everyone will hear us and think it's time for lunch."

"We're billowing flames and smoke like a dragon!"
F.E. laughed as he pushed up the throttle a little
more. "But it feels as if we're riding on air!"

"Or sliding down a snowbank on a sled!" F.O.
shouted. "Or flying like an arrow from a bow!"

Every dog in town came running to bark and howl
at the strange-looking "thing." Horses were
frightened. One broke from its buggy and dashed
away as fast as it could go. People rushed from
buildings all along the street to see what was making
the noise.

"Get that thing off the street before someone gets
hurt!" a man shouted angrily, shaking his fist at the
twins.

"There's no substitute for a horse!" someone
called loudly.

"Mama, look! A giant teakettle is coming down
the street!" a small boy cried.

They brought the buggy to a stop. F.E. told the
crowd that though the buggy was indeed loud, it was
safe. No one believed him.

"Why, it's frightening just to look at," said one woman who had been riding a bicycle.

"That bulky thing will never take the place of the horse!" a man said.

When the twins reached home, F.E. said, "We can invent a better buggy than this."

"I believe we can build a better one and a faster one, too," said F.O., pulling at his beard. "But this time we'll make our own engine and boiler."

The twins went to work. They bought parts. Then they worked long and hard to build an engine and a boiler that would lighten the load of the buggy. When they had finished, the new steam buggy did not whistle quite so loudly as the first. They called this new buggy a "steam car."

F.O. and F.E. had so much fun with their steam car that they decided to build another one. The second car moved a little faster than the first. With the two cars, they would often ride down the street side by side.

People thought their eyes were playing tricks on them when they saw the two men and the two cars. F.O. and F.E. looked alike in matching coats and caps. The strange cars they were driving also looked alike!

In time, other automobiles were invented. Some were powered by gas, and some were powered by electricity. There were still very few power-driven cars in the country.

When the first automobile show was held, F.E. and F.O. entered their steam car. People at the show were very excited about the design of the new car.

"Mr. Stanley, please sell me your steam car," said a tall man in a top hat. "I will pay anything you ask for it."

The twins had never discussed the subject of selling their cars. However, many people wanted to buy them. So the twins went home, bought an old bicycle factory, and started making cars. They called them Stanley Steamers. Because of the way they billowed steam, the cars earned the nickname "Teakettles."

The twins raced their cars at many country fairs. They often won the races and their names became well known. Before long, they had to build a much bigger factory.

"You know, F.O.," said F.E. one day, "our cars travel fast, but they don't look very fast."

"Well, that's true," F.O. agreed. "They are bulky, but they don't have to be."

The next car they designed looked more like a racing car. It was shaped something like a submarine. Years later, this car was nicknamed the "Rocket."

The Rocket broke the world's speed record in 1906, at the races in Ormond Beach, Florida. It went 127 miles an hour. The driver, Fred Mariott, was the first person in the world to travel two miles a minute.

"This car can travel much faster than that," said F.O. "Let's come back to the races next year and break our own record."

F.O. and F.E. returned to Ormond Beach in 1907 with Fred Mariott and the "Rocket." The white sand of the beach was covered with cars of all shapes and sizes, driven by gas, electricity, and steam.

"Here we go for three miles a minute!" Fred Mariott shouted as the race began. He pushed up the throttle. Before anyone could say, "There goes the flying teakettle!" the little car was out of sight.

The speed was up to 150 miles an hour and still climbing. Suddenly the car hit a small bump. At that speed, even a small bump means danger. The car was lifted high into the air. When the Rocket fell, it broke into a hundred pieces.

Fred was hurt in the accident. Later, when he was well again, he often told the tale of the great race. But the accident made the twins sad.

"We did it, F.O.," said F.E. "We built the fastest car in the world."

"It was too fast to stay on the ground, F.E.," F.O. added.

"It's exciting to race the fastest car in the world, but because of Fred's accident, we'll never race again," F.E. said.

And they never did.

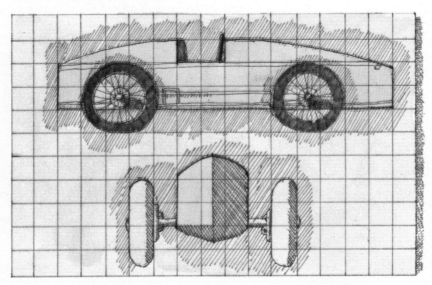

1. Where did the Stanley brothers get the idea of putting a steam engine inside a buggy to make it go faster?

2. What did people think when they first saw the Stanley brothers riding down the street in their buggy?

3. What did the Stanley brothers do to make a better buggy?

4. How was the Stanley brothers' steam car different from other cars being made at that time?

5. Why did the Stanley brothers decide to stop racing their steam car?

6. Long ago, people often laughed at new inventions. Now, people don't laugh so much at new inventions. Why do you suppose that is?

POPCORN

For almost a week a freezing rain had fallen on the little town of Bloom's Crossing. The farmers who lived near the town were worried. Their fields were covered with ice, and their animals were cold. Even Mr. Moto, who ran a little food store, was worried.

"This storm had better end soon," he told his daughter, Joyce. "If the farmers lose money, then so will we."

While Joyce and her father talked, a big truck pulled up outside the store. "It's Katy," said Joyce. "She must be delivering the popcorn that Mrs. Smith ordered."

A few minutes later, Katy came in wheeling a tall stack of wooden boxes. "Where do you want

these ten cases of popcorn?" she asked. "And there are ten more on the truck."

Mr. Moto looked at Joyce. "Twenty *cases*? Why would Mrs. Smith want twenty cases of popcorn?"

"I don't know," said Joyce. "She slipped the order under the door one night after we had closed."

"Well, I hope Mrs. Smith has some use for them," said Katy. "This company won't take anything back once it's delivered."

When Katy left, Joyce and Mr. Moto loaded the wooden boxes onto their truck. They then drove to Mrs. Smith's farm. When they got there, Mrs. Smith was standing in the yard holding two chairs.

"Where do you want your twenty cases of popcorn?" Mr. Moto called.

"Twenty cases?" said Mrs. Smith. "I ordered twenty cans."

"Oh!" said Joyce. "The word *can* looked like *cases* to me."

Mr. Moto didn't say a word. His friendship with Mrs. Smith went back a long way. He would just have to pay for the popcorn and try to sell it to someone else.

Joyce looked at the chairs that Mrs. Smith was holding. "What are you going to do with those chairs?"

"I'm going to burn them," said Mrs. Smith.

"What for?" asked Joyce. "They look like good chairs to me."

"I need wood to get a fire going," said Mrs. Smith. "These chairs are all I have. My chickens are freezing, and there's not a dry stick of wood for fifty miles around."

Joyce and her father followed Mrs. Smith into the shed where she kept her chickens. An old stove stood empty and cold in one corner of the shed. Shivering chickens were perched everywhere.

"See what I mean?" said Mrs. Smith. "Even if I could find some wood, I couldn't get it here soon enough. These birds won't last much longer."

Mrs. Smith picked up an ax and got ready to break up the chairs. "I don't mind telling you," she said, "that this storm is really a hardship for me. I paid a lot of money for these chairs."

"I wish I could help," said Mr. Moto. "But I have my share of hardships, too. We have a truck full of popcorn that nobody wants."

When Joyce heard her father say *popcorn*, her eyes lit up. "Popcorn!" she shouted. "It's the answer to your problem, Father. And to Mrs. Smith's problem, too."

"It is?" said Mr. Moto.

"It is?" said Mrs. Smith, putting down her ax.

"Don't you see?" asked Joyce. "If Mrs. Smith buys the popcorn, she can heat the shed."

Mrs. Smith and Mr. Moto both looked very puzzled. They were thinking about what would happen if Mrs. Smith put twenty cases of popcorn into the stove!

Mr. Moto shook his head. "No, Joyce. Mrs. Smith needs wood, not popcorn."

"I don't mean the popcorn itself," said Joyce. "I mean the cases that the cans are packed in. Don't you remember? They're made of wood."

Now it was Mrs. Smith's and Mr. Moto's turn to smile. "How many cases do you have?" asked Mrs. Smith.

"Twenty," said Mr. Moto.

"All you have to do is buy the popcorn," said Joyce. "We'll throw in the cases for free—won't we, Father?"

"Is it a deal?" Mr. Moto asked Mrs. Smith.

"It's a deal," said Mrs. Smith.

A little while later, Mrs. Smith, Mr. Moto, and Joyce watched the flames roar up inside the stove. The shed was warm as toast, and all the chickens looked happy. Mr. Moto was glad that his friendship with Mrs. Smith had been saved.

"You know what I'd like right now?" asked Mrs. Smith.

"Some *popcorn!*" said Joyce and Mr. Moto.

1. What was the error that Joyce made with Mrs. Smith's order for popcorn?

2. How was Mrs. Smith planning to keep her chickens warm?

3. What was Joyce's idea for helping Mrs. Smith?

4. How did Joyce's idea also help her father work out his problem?

5. Did Mrs. Smith burn the popcorn along with the wooden cases?

6. Do you think this story could really happen? Why or why not?

7. Think of two other ways that Joyce could have helped Mrs. Smith with her problem. Make one way silly and the other way serious.

Basketballs and Bells

Maria Sanchez was always very busy. Early in the morning she delivered newspapers. During the day she went to school. In the afternoon she played basketball for the Circle City Flyers.

Every morning, with the last stars of night still twinkling overhead, Maria rode her bike through the quiet streets. She took careful aim as she threw the papers onto porches and front steps.

Maria liked delivering papers, but she liked basketball even better. She was one of the best players on her team and she never missed a game.

One afternoon, while Maria was changing into her basketball clothes, she got a call from Anita Bell. Ms. Bell was the owner of Bell's Diner.

"I haven't been getting my paper," said Ms. Bell. "I think a dog has been picking it up from the steps."

"I'm sorry," said Maria.

"I'm sorry, too," said Ms. Bell. "My customers enjoy reading the paper while they're eating breakfast. I'd like to have one every morning for

them. From now on, please put the paper where the dog can't get it.''

The next morning, when Maria got to the big bell in front of Bell's Diner, she got off her bike.

''I have to find a safe place to leave the paper,'' she said to herself.

Maria looked all around the diner, but she couldn't find a place to put the newspaper. Finally, she threw it onto the roof.

"The dog won't get the paper up there," thought Maria, as she rode off.

On her way home from school that day, Maria stopped by to see Ms. Bell.

"Did you get your paper this morning?" asked Maria.

"How could I get it?" said Ms. Bell, looking very upset. "It was up on the roof. As a matter of fact, it's still there."

"Well, I didn't want the dog to get it," said Maria. "There wasn't any other place I could safely put it."

"It's true that the dog didn't get it," said Ms. Bell. "But I didn't get it either. You'll have to bring me another paper."

"Can I bring it to you tomorrow?" asked Maria. "I have to play basketball now."

"I don't want today's paper tomorrow," said Ms. Bell. "My customers want to see the paper today. If I don't have a paper for them, I'm afraid they'll stop eating here."

So, Maria had to go down to the newspaper office and pick up another paper. By the time she dropped off the paper at Bell's Diner, it was too late for her to play basketball.

"If I bring you the paper every afternoon," Maria told Ms. Bell, "I won't have time to play basketball. But the team needs me. We'll have to think of something else."

Ms. Bell and Maria thought about their problem for a long time. Finally, Ms. Bell said, "I have it! From now on, when you deliver the paper, ring the big bell in front of the diner. That way I can wake up and get the paper before the dog gets it."

"That sounds like a fine plan," said Maria. "I'm sure it will work."

"It had better work," said Ms. Bell. "My customers are getting more and more unhappy. I don't know how much longer they'll continue to eat at Bell's Diner without a morning paper to read."

Early the next morning, Maria rode out with a big load of newspapers. When she reached Bell's Diner, she threw the paper on the steps. Then she rang the bell as loud as she could. She rang it so loud, in fact, that it rattled windows from one end of the street to the other.

For three days in a row, Maria delivered the paper to Bell's Diner. For three days in a row, she rang the bell. Best of all, for three days in a row, Maria didn't hear once from Ms. Bell.

"Ms. Bell's plan must be working," thought Maria. "At last my afternoons are free for basketball."

Then, on the fourth day, Maria saw Ms. Bell sitting outside her diner. She looked very unhappy.

"Maria, I want to talk to you," said Ms. Bell. "I have a terrible problem."

Maria felt her heart sink. "Oh, no!" she thought. "Her problem must have something to do with the paper."

Sure enough, Ms. Bell said, "I'm afraid I will have to stop the paper. There's a chance that I'll also have to shut down my diner."

Maria looked at Ms. Bell. "Why?" she asked.

"It's my neighbors," sighed Ms. Bell. "They say that the bell wakes them up every morning. They made me promise it would never ring again. Without the bell, I can't get the paper. Without the paper, I can't keep my customers happy."

"I'm sorry about the paper," said Maria. "Is there anything else we can do? I don't want you to have to close the diner."

"Maybe you could bring me the paper in the afternoon," said Ms. Bell.

"But I told you that if I do that, I won't be able to play basketball," said Maria. "And basketball is my. . ."

Suddenly, Maria stopped, and her eyes lit up.

"Basketball!" she shouted. "Why, that's it! Why didn't I think of that before?"

Ms. Bell stared at Maria. "Basketball?" she said. "What does that have to do with my paper?"

"Everything," smiled Maria, walking over to the big iron bell and turning it upside down. "You see, your bell is going to be my basket."

"What a wonderful idea," said Ms. Bell.

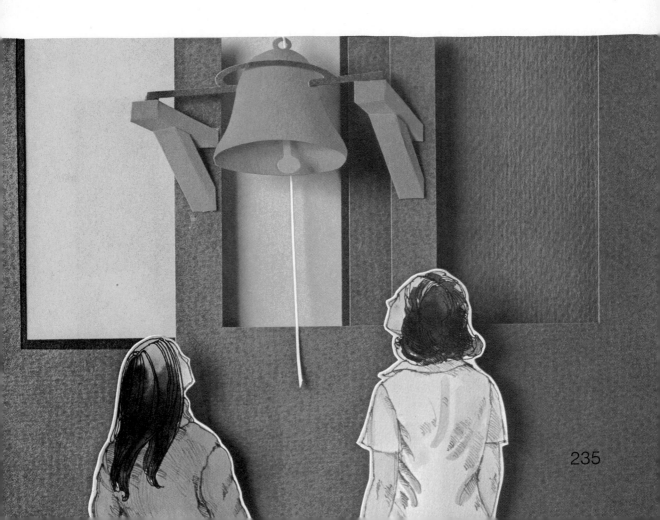

"All you have to do is turn the bell upside down every night," said Maria. "If you do that, I promise that every morning your customers will have their paper to read while they have breakfast."

The next morning, Maria loaded up her papers and rode out into the dawn. She hurried through the streets of her town, tossing papers onto porches and front steps. When she got to Bell's Diner, she took aim at the upside-down bell and let the paper fly. Whoosh! The paper sailed right into the bell.

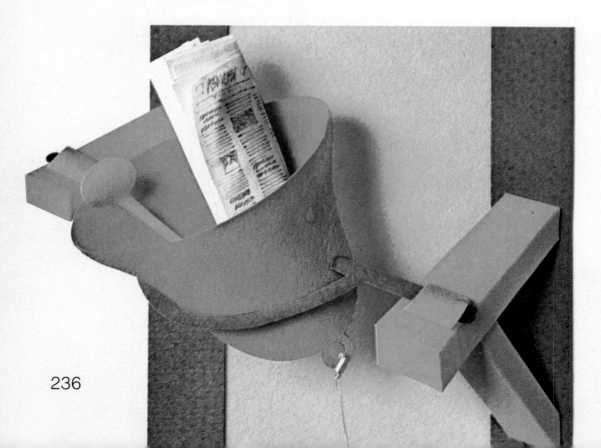

"Thanks to that bell, Ms. Bell will get her paper every day," said Maria as she rode away. "Of course, I'll get something, too," she thought. "From now on I'll get to play basketball not only in the afternoon, but in the morning, too!"

THINK ABOUT IT

1. One afternoon, Maria Sanchez got a call from Anita Bell. What did Ms. Bell say had been happening to her paper?

2. After Maria's first plan didn't work, what did Ms. Bell tell Maria to do when she delivered the paper every morning? Why didn't this plan work out very well?

3. What plan for delivering the paper finally did work out?

4. What might have happened if Maria and Ms. Bell had not come up with a plan that worked?

5. Which was more important to Maria—delivering papers or playing basketball? How do you know?

6. If you had been Maria, how would you have worked out the problem?

KEEP TRACK

Maria Sanchez in "Basketballs and Bells" played basketball for the Circle City Flyers. She kept a record for a week of the number of baskets she made during each practice game. In that way, Maria was able to check on how well she was playing. At the end of one week, this is the record she had.

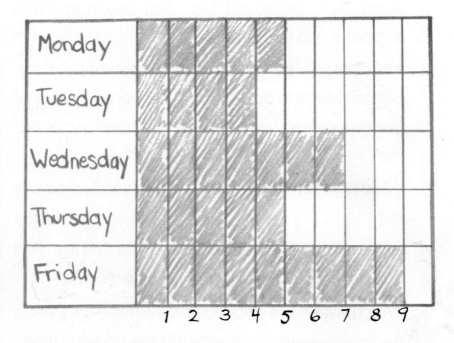

This record is a special kind of drawing called a "bar graph." It is used to show facts in a way that

238

makes them clearer and easier to understand. The left side of the bar graph on the previous page shows the days of the week Maria played. The numerals at the bottom of the graph stand for the number of baskets she made in each game. To find out how well Maria did each day, read across each shaded bar on the graph. Then read down to the numeral at the bottom. In Monday's game, for example, Maria made five baskets.

Now look at the bar graph again and answer the following questions.

1. How many days did Maria play during the week?
2. Which day did Maria make the most baskets? How many baskets did she make that day?
3. Which day did Maria make the fewest baskets? How many baskets did she make that day?

Keep a record of how well you do in a game you like to play. Use a bar graph to show the facts. Or, if you like, keep a record of a favorite player on a real team.

240

My Dog Is a Plumber

My dog is a plumber; he must be a boy.

Although I must tell you his favorite toy

Is a little play stove with pans and with pots

Which he really must like, 'cause he plays
    with it lots.

So perhaps he's a girl, which kind of makes
    sense,

Since he can't throw a ball and he can't
    climb a fence.

But neither can Dad, and I know *he's* a man,

And Mom is a woman, and *she* drives a van.

Maybe the problem is in trying to tell

Just what someone is by what he does well.

Dan Greenburg

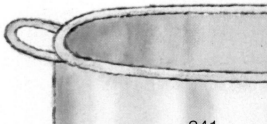

241

six

Use Your Head, Tom

"Wait for me, Tom!"

Tom Bluewater turned around and waited as his friend George came running along the street. Most of the time Tom was glad to see George, but today he had promised to run some errands. Since the day they'd met, George had always been able to make Tom play instead of work.

Right now, George was greeting Tom, saying, "Let's go have some fun!"

I'll see you after a while, George," Tom said. "I've got some important things to do this afternoon."

George snorted. "Important things! You mean errands in the neighborhood!"

"Yes," Tom said. "But they are important. I'm earning money to take my mother to the movies tonight. Besides, I promised Mrs. Able that I'd help her."

"Isn't your father back yet?" George asked.

"No, he's on another trip for his company. This time he had to fly to the coast."

Tom did not like to talk about his father's trips. He missed his father too much. Sometimes he wished his family had never come to this great city that had changed their lives. They should have stayed in the north, in the childhood home of his parents.

"Can't your mother watch a movie on television tonight?" George asked.

"Sure. But she likes to go out once in a while," Tom said. "And so do I. It's important to both of us."

He thought of his mother's big smile when he had asked her about the movies. Her dark eyes had flashed. "We will have a good time!" she had exclaimed.

Tom said again, "It's important."

"Well, look, Tom," George said, "I've got a better idea. Let's go up to the park and look around the zoo for a while. We won't stay long." He pulled Tom's hair down over his eyes.

Tom grabbed George and wrestled him to the sidewalk, laughing and yelling. A scowling man had to step around them.

A few moments later George stood up. "There comes the bus," he said, puffing. "Come on. Let's go, Tom. You can't work all the time." He took off at a run.

"George is right," Tom thought. "I can go to the park for a little while. There's no harm in having a little fun."

"Tom!"

It was Mrs. Able. She was leaning out of her front window. "You didn't forget, did you, Tom?" she called. "You were going to help me this afternoon. Don't you remember?"

"Oh, I didn't forget, Mrs. Able," Tom said. "I'll be back to help you later on." He glanced toward the bus, which had come to a stop at the corner.

"Come on!" George yelled. "Next stop—the park!"

Tom ran to the corner and jumped on the bus. His promise to Mrs. Able was a troublesome thought that he pushed from his mind. He looked out the bus window as the busy life on the streets sped past them. Then he took a worn little sketch pad and a pencil from his pocket and looked around the bus. Soon he began to sketch a man with a long shaggy beard who sat across from him.

"Let's see," George said. "Say, that's very good, Tom. Do you carry that drawing pad around with you all the time?"

"Mostly all the time," Tom said.

At Fifty-Ninth Street, the bus came to a stop. Tom followed George to the zoo, which was just beyond some brick buildings. As if greeting them, a lion's roar shook the lion house. "This is great!" Tom exclaimed. "I wouldn't miss this for anything."

Inside the lion house, the air was warm and stuffy. Tom walked slowly, wondering at the slanted yellow cat eyes that followed him in silence. He paused in front of one cage and started sketching a shaggy lion that was studying him.

But George was in a hurry. "Come on," he said, grabbing Tom's arm. The pencil skipped across the paper. "Come on, Tom."

George made a big thing out of buying a box of popcorn. For a long time they roamed the paths of the park. Then through the trees, they saw a rowboat glittering on the lake.

"Come on," George said. "Let's go!" They sped to the landing where the boats rocked in the water. Tom wondered how much it would cost to rent one. He jingled the coins in his pocket. No! He would need that money for bus fare home.

Home! He glanced at his own shadow stretching long in front of him. Out on the lake there were many long shadows. Long shadows! Was the sun that low? Tom looked and saw the purple light of dusk through the trees. The day was gone!

It was a long ride home on the bus. Tom tried not to think about his promises to Mrs. Able and to his mother. He knew he didn't have time to earn enough money to go to the movies.

"George is right," Tom thought. "We can watch a movie on TV." But he knew that TV was no substitute for going out.

At last he saw the dark brick buildings of his neighborhood ahead in the dusk. He did not look at George when he said "So long" and headed down the block for home.

He climbed the stairs, pausing at his door. "It's no use waiting," he told himself. "I've got to tell her. Maybe I can make it sound all right."

Tom opened the door. His mother was singing a happy song. He sank into a chair, looked at the floor, and took a deep breath. "We can't go to the movies," he said. "I'm sorry. I have no money."

His mother seemed surprised. Then she began to fix their supper. When they were at the table she put her arm around Tom. "This will be a good evening," she said. "We can watch TV, and you can make some popcorn."

Tom did not feel like eating. He poked at his food. He half listened as his mother talked about the plans they would make when his father came home. "Oh!" she said suddenly. "I just remembered something. Mrs. Feinberg told me that her artist friend is coming tomorrow. She wants you to bring your sketches up for her friend to look at. They especially want to see the one you did on brotherhood —the one of all our neighbors laughing together."

A long time ago, Mrs. Feinberg, their upstairs neighbor, had promised to let Tom show his sketches and drawings to her artist friend. "Well," thought Tom, "some people are good at keeping their promises."

Then he smiled at his mother. "That's great!" he said. "I'll ask how I can get to be a real artist."

Tom sat up straight. "But first," he said, "I'll do the work for Mrs. Able if she will still let me. *Then* I'll see about being an artist. It is important to keep a promise."

Suddenly he was hungry. "This is the best supper
in the world, Mom," he said. "And tomorrow night,
I'll be the cook. That's a promise!"

THINK ABOUT IT

1. At the beginning of the story, George wanted Tom to play. Why didn't Tom want to play?

2. How did George get Tom to play instead of doing his errands?

3. How did Tom know that he had played too long in the park?

4. How did Tom's mother feel about not being able to go to the movies? How do you know?

5. What happened that made Tom decide to try to keep his promises to people?

6. Have you ever let anyone down? How did it make you feel? Has anyone ever let *you* down?

Su Ling's Arrow

In the village of Ten Wing, on the banks of a far-off river, lived a girl named Su Ling. Every morning Su Ling could be found by the river shooting her bow and arrow. Su Ling was a very good shot, and she worked hard to become even better. More than anything, she wanted to become a member of the Ten Wing bow and arrow team. Every year the Ten Wing team went down the river to the village of Wan Shu to shoot against the Wan Shu team. Someday Su Ling hoped to be picked to make the trip to Wan Shu.

When Su Ling was still very young, she went to see Mr. Bin, the head of the Ten Wing team. "I want to go to Wan Shu tomorrow," said Su Ling. "I want to be on the team."

Mr. Bin shook his head. "You are too young," he said. "Wait a few more years until you are stronger. Then you can go."

"Please," begged Su Ling. "Take me with you. I can shoot as well as anyone in Ten Wing."

"I am sorry," said Mr. Bin. "You must wait."

"If I can't shoot with the team, at least let me come along," begged Su Ling. "There must be *something* I can do to help the team."

Mr. Bin thought for a long time. At last he said, "All right, Su Ling. You can help us with the scoring."

Su Ling wished she had been put on the team, but she was not unhappy. At least she would have a chance to help the Ten Wing team.

"The boat leaves early tomorrow morning," said Mr. Bin. "Don't be late."

At dawn the next morning a large crowd gathered on the banks of the river. They had all come out to wish the team good luck. Su Ling climbed into the boat with Mr. Bin and the team.

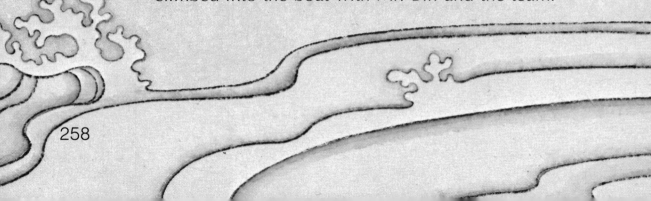

"Su Ling is going to help us with the scoring," Mr. Bin explained. "Perhaps she will also bring us the luck we need to win today."

The team untied the ropes that held the little boat to shore. Then the crowd helped to push them away into the river.

"Good luck!" shouted the people on shore. "May all your arrows find their mark!"

The little boat had two paddles. Mai Sun, the oldest team member, took one of them, and Mr. Bin took the other. They paddled down the river toward Wan Shu.

Su Ling sat in the back of the boat and watched the deep blue waters of the river slip by. After a while she reached down and touched her bow, which lay at her feet.

"Someday," she promised herself, "I will be going to Wan Shu not just as a helper. I will be going as a member of the team."

For more than an hour the boat slid gently through the waters of the river. After a while, however, the water began to move faster. The little boat picked up speed. From time to time sharp rocks appeared in the river, and Mai Sun and Mr. Bin had to paddle carefully around them.

"Rainbow Falls are coming up," said Mr. Bin. "Soon we will have to take the boat out of the water and carry it around the falls. If we went over the falls in this boat, we'd be smashed to pieces."

The closer the boat drifted toward the falls, the meaner the river became. The water swirled and churned. It slapped against the sharp rocks and filled the air with a glittering mist. Then, all at once, Su Ling heard a thundering roar. It was Rainbow Falls.

"Head for the shore," shouted Mai Sun. "The falls are not far away!"

As they turned for the shore, the boat brushed against a rock. The rock lifted one side of the boat out of the water. When the boat came down, Su Ling heard Mr. Bin shout. "My paddle!" he cried. "I've lost my paddle!"

Su Ling could see the paddle bobbing near the boat. Mr. Bin tried to grab for it, but it stayed just out of his reach.

"Now we're in real trouble," Mr. Bin cried. "With only one paddle, we'll never get to shore."

Mai Sun paddled with all her might, but she was no match for the swirling waters of the river. There was nothing anyone could do. It seemed as if nothing could keep the little boat from moving nearer to the falls.

As the falls came closer and closer, Su Ling noticed a pile of string on the floor of the boat. She reached for the string and quickly picked out an arrow with a very sharp tip.

When Mr. Bin saw Su Ling taking out her arrow, he looked puzzled. "What are you doing?" he shouted. "This is no time to be playing."

"I'm not playing," said Su Ling. "I'm trying to get the paddle back. Please, everybody, hold the boat steady. I have to stand up." As she spoke, she tied the string to the arrow.

Su Ling picked up her bow. Then, she stood up slowly and carefully. She put the arrow in her bow and took careful aim at the bobbing paddle.

"Sit down!" shouted Mr. Bin, who still didn't know what Su Ling was doing. "Sit down or you'll tip the boat over."

263

Su Ling was not listening to Mr. Bin. There was only one thing on her mind. She wanted to hit the paddle with her arrow, and she wanted to hit it on the first shot.

Su Ling aimed her arrow carefully. Just at the right second, she sent it out across the churning foam. It was a perfect shot. The arrow slammed into the worn wood of the paddle and stuck. Quickly, Su Ling pulled in the paddle like a fish on a line. Mr. Bin grabbed it the second it reached the boat. Then he and Mai Sun began paddling for the shore with all their might. Inch by inch and foot by foot, the boat made its way through the swirling waters. At last, tired but happy, the Ten Wing team reached the safety of the shore.

As soon as everyone was safely on shore, Mr. Bin thanked Su Ling for saving the boat.

"That was the most beautiful shot I have ever seen," he said. "You have more than proved that you are a good shot. We want you to be a member of the team. With you on our side, I know we will beat the Wan Shu team."

Su Ling's heart filled with joy.

"Thank you," she said. "I'll shoot well today, I promise. I'll make you all proud."

"You've already made us proud," said Mr. Bin.

THINK ABOUT IT

1. At the beginning of the story, what was it that Su Ling wanted more than anything?

2. Why was Su Ling able to go with the team?

3. How did Su Ling save the boat in which she and the team were traveling?

4. How did Mr. Bin reward Su Ling?

5. Do you think Su Ling knew she would be made a member of the team if she saved the boat?

6. How do you think the rest of the team felt about Su Ling's being made a member?

7. Has anyone ever told you that you were still too young to do something? How did you feel? What did you do?

Professor Coconut and the Thief

It all started when the cook's hat disappeared. Sipo and I couldn't figure it out. I'm Peter. Sipo is my friend. We're both eight, and we go to school together here in Africa. Ever since school got out for the summer, Sipo and I have been helping the cook. Until the other day, we never saw his head. He always wore a hat.

Then one morning, the hat was gone.

Sipo had come early that morning to deliver the eggs. Sipo raises chickens and sells their eggs to our cook. "Where is your hat?" Sipo asked.

"It disappeared," said the cook.

"How?" asked Sipo.

The cook shook his head. "I don't know," he said. "It just disappeared."

The next day my hammer disappeared. I was getting ready to go to Sipo's. He lives with his grandmother and his monkey, Kima. We had to fix up some holes in Sipo's chicken house. I needed my hammer, and it was gone.

The day after that, Professor Albert's pen disappeared. Professor Albert is the head of our group of scientists. My mother is a scientist. She came to Africa to dig for bones of animals and people who lived a very long time ago.

Professor Albert is very forgetful. One day, when he was wearing his shirt inside out for the third day in a row, Sipo said, "I think there is coconut milk in his head instead of a brain." After that we called him Professor Coconut.

The day the pen disappeared, Professor Coconut ran out of his hut shouting, "Everyone out. *Everyone out!*"

Everyone came running out of the tents.

"My pen is gone. Do you hear me?" he shouted. Hear him? Even the elephants at the water hole a mile away could hear him. "If my pen is not returned before breakfast is over, I will, I will. . . ." He started to walk away. His pen never did show up.

Sipo and I talked about the missing things that afternoon. "Maybe *we* can catch the thief," Sipo said.

"How are we going to do that?" I asked.

"We'll set a trap by Professor Coconut's hut," said Sipo. "The thief was there last night. Maybe he will come again tonight."

"Professor Coconut locks the door every night," I said. "So the thief must have come in through the window. That's where we have to make the trap."

"Good thinking!" said Sipo. Then he looked up at the sky and breathed deeply. "It is going to rain tonight," he said.

I looked up. The sky was clear and blue. "But this is the dry season," I said.

"Tonight it will rain," said Sipo. If Sipo said it was going to rain, it was going to rain. He knew about those things.

"We will dig a hole under the window. The hole will fill up with water. The thief will step in it." Sipo smiled and continued. "Tomorrow the thief will have to put his shoes out in the sun to dry. We will know who the thief is when we see his shoes."

As soon as it got dark, we dug our hole. Then Sipo went home, and we left the rest to the rain.

All night long I could hear the rain, but in the morning the sun was out. I raced around the camp, looking for shoes drying in the sun. I didn't find any. No thief had come, I thought. So I went to breakfast.

As I was eating my eggs, Professor Coconut stormed into the tent. He was wearing his tie on top of his pajamas. "The thief is back," he shouted. "He took my watch!" Then Professor Coconut turned to me. "And *you.* You come with me."

He marched me to the door of his hut and pointed inside. The hole had filled with water, all right. And the water had overflowed into the hut. He stared at me. "Did you do this?" he shouted.

I groaned. I wanted to tell him I was sorry, but he went inside and slammed the door.

When I told Sipo about the missing watch, he shook his head. "How did the thief get in without getting his shoes wet? We must try another trap."

"OK. But it had better be a good one."

We sat down to think.

Sipo jumped up. "I know! I once read about how you can track footprints by sprinkling flour on the ground. How about that?"

"That's a great idea," I said.

We raced to the cook's tent, where the cook gave us a bag of flour. Then we built a hideout. We cut some branches and stuck them into the ground and then filled in the spaces with more branches. When we finished, we tried it out. It was perfect.

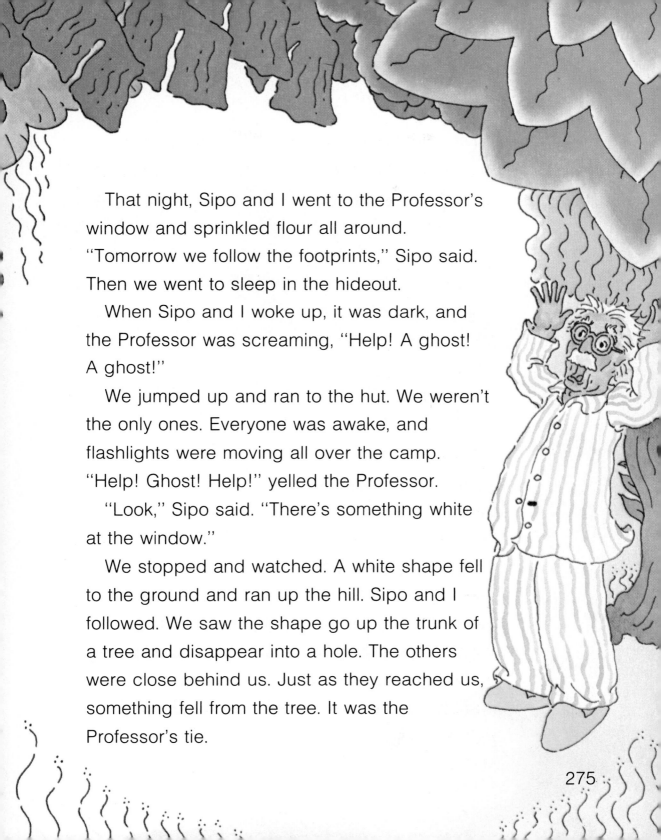

That night, Sipo and I went to the Professor's window and sprinkled flour all around. "Tomorrow we follow the footprints," Sipo said. Then we went to sleep in the hideout.

When Sipo and I woke up, it was dark, and the Professor was screaming, "Help! A ghost! A ghost!"

We jumped up and ran to the hut. We weren't the only ones. Everyone was awake, and flashlights were moving all over the camp. "Help! Ghost! Help!" yelled the Professor.

"Look," Sipo said. "There's something white at the window."

We stopped and watched. A white shape fell to the ground and ran up the hill. Sipo and I followed. We saw the shape go up the trunk of a tree and disappear into a hole. The others were close behind us. Just as they reached us, something fell from the tree. It was the Professor's tie.

Everyone looked up. Kima was sitting on a branch. The cook's hat was on her head. The Professor's pen was in her mouth. His watch was on her arm. And my hammer was in her paw.

I looked at Sipo. Sipo looked at me. Of course! Kima was the thief! Only a monkey could have gotten through our traps without being caught.

Sipo started to laugh. I tried to say something, but I couldn't—I was laughing too hard. Everyone else was laughing, too. Everyone but the Professor. He was putting on his tie.

THINK ABOUT IT

1. The setting of this story is Africa. How did Peter happen to be in Africa?

2. Who was Sipo? Who was Kima?

3. What was the first thing that disappeared? What other things disappeared?

4. Who had taken all of these things?

5. How did the boys plan to catch the thief? Why didn't their plans work?

6. Were there any clues in the story as to who the thief was?

7. What made Professor Coconut think he was seeing a ghost in his window?

8. How would you have tried to catch the thief?

CUT-UPS

What's a cut-up? It's a picture or design created out of cut paper. It is easy to make one from several sheets of bright construction paper. You'll also need one sheet of black construction paper, one sheet of white paper, a pencil, glue, and scissors. The next two pages will give you directions. Be sure to read them carefully before you begin.

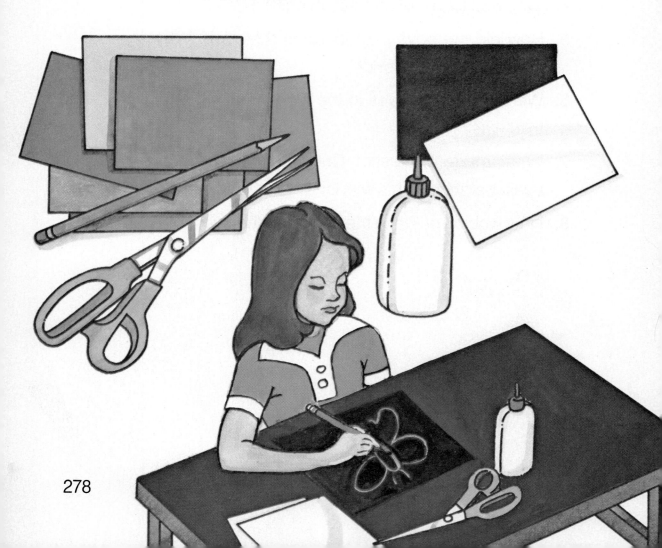

First you must decide on a design. When you plan your cut-up, choose a design with large areas that can be filled in with small pieces of colored paper. A butterfly, a clown, or a rainbow would be a good choice. Keep your design in mind as you sketch its outline on the sheet of black construction paper.

Cut the colored sheets of paper into ½-inch strips. Then cut each strip into small squares. Cut some of the squares in half from corner to corner to make triangles.

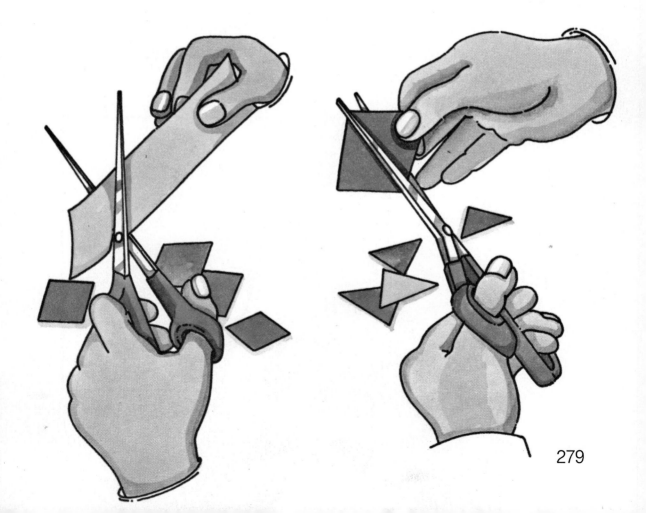

Each small square and triangle must be glued onto your design, one by one. Some of the black background should show between the pieces. The effect you create with color is up to you. A clown might have a red suit with yellow dots, while a butterfly would look pretty with a mixture of colors.

Once all the pieces have been glued in place, cut out your design. Leave a black edge showing all around it. Then glue the design onto the white construction paper.

Cut-ups can be hung, used as place mats, or made into greeting cards. They are always different looking and beautiful.

Evan's Corner

Evan walked home from school slowly. A bright red flower on a windowsill caught his eye. "That flower has its own pot," he thought. "I wish *I* had a place of my own."

He crossed a noisy, busy street and turned into the building where he lived. He walked up the steep stairway to the two rooms that he and his brothers and sisters and parents shared. "I sure have a lot of family," Evan thought. "And no place to call just *mine*."

Most days Evan was the first one home. But today the door flew open before he touched it.

"Surprise!" His mother stood there laughing. "My boss said I could leave early."

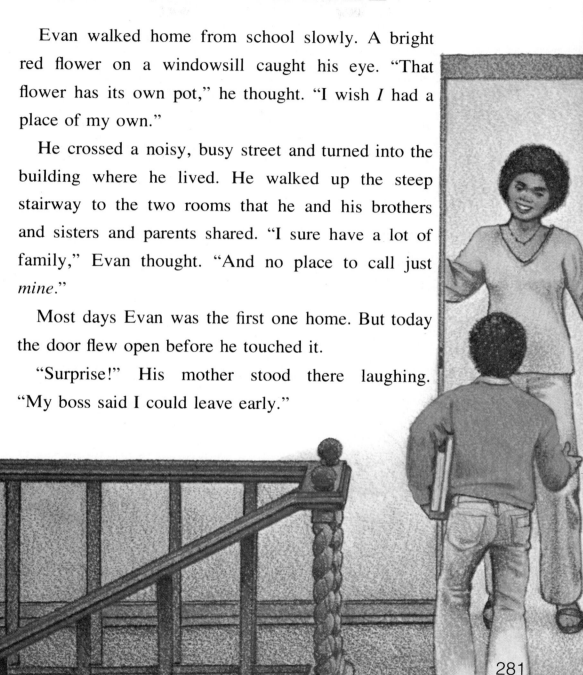

Evan gave his mother a big hug. "Mama, you know what I've been wishing for *hard*?"

"Tell me." His mother smiled.

Evan told her about the flower and its pot. Then he said, "*I* want a place of my own."

His mother thought and thought. Her face lighted up. "There are eight of us," she said. "That means each one of us can have a corner! You have first choice, Evan."

Evan ran to every corner of the rooms. The one he wanted for his own had a nice small window and a bit of shiny floor.

"This is mine," Evan said happily.

That night before dinner he sat alone on the floor, in his corner. His little brother Adam asked him, "Why do you want a corner of your own, Evan?"

Evan thought for a minute. "I want a chance to be lonely," he said.

Adam tiptoed away and left him.

After supper there were jobs to do. When Evan's work was done, he sat in his corner again. He looked out the window.

Adam came behind Evan and said softly, "Are you being lonely now?"

"No," Evan answered. "I'm wasting time."

Adam asked, "Can I ever come into your corner, Evan?"

"Why don't you choose a corner of your own?" Evan said.

Adam's choice was the corner across the room from Evan's. But Adam didn't know what to do in his corner. After a minute he left and played horse with his big sister Susan.

The next morning, as soon as he woke up, Evan ran to his corner. His bit of shiny floor was as bright as ever. His window was still fun to look through. But Evan felt that his corner needed something more.

He stared at the bare walls. "I need a picture!" he thought. "And I'll make it myself!"

In school Evan painted a picture of the sea with big blue waves and a green boat.

As soon as he got home from school, Evan taped the picture to the wall beside the window in his corner. It looked just right.

When Adam came home with their biggest sister, Helen, he went right to Evan's corner. "That's pretty, Evan!" he said. "Do you think I could draw a picture for my corner?"

"Sure you could," Evan told him.

Adam ran off. But he could not find any paper or crayons. He returned to Evan.

"Are you wasting time, Evan?" Adam asked softly.

"No," Evan told him. "I'm enjoying peace and quiet." Adam tiptoed off.

That night Evan lay awake in bed, thinking about his corner. He remembered the red flower in its pot. He thought, "I need a plant!"

On Saturday, Evan went to the playground with a
glass and a spoon. He found a weed that had big,
lacy flowers on it. He dug it up with his spoon and
planted it in the glass. Then he took it home and put
it on the windowsill in his corner.

Now Evan had many things. He had a place of his
own. He could be lonely there. He could waste time
if he liked. He could enjoy peace and quiet. But—it
was strange. He just wasn't happy.

When his mother came home that evening, Evan
said, "Mama, I'm not happy in my corner. What do
I need now?"

Together she and Evan stood off from the corner and looked at it. Evan's corner was beautiful. They both saw that.

"Evan," his mother said finally, "maybe you need to leave your corner for a while. Just fixing it up isn't enough." She smiled at him. "Maybe you need to step out now and help someone else." She left Evan alone in his corner to think it over.

Adam came in. "Are you enjoying peace and quiet, Evan?" he asked.

"No," Evan said slowly, "I'm planning to borrow Susan's crayons."

"Why?"

"To help you draw a picture if you want to. I'm planning to help you fix up your corner. We'll make it the most wonderful corner in the whole world!"

Joy spread over Adam's face — and over Evan's.

They ran across the room together to work on Adam's corner.

THINK ABOUT IT

1. At the beginning of the story, what did Evan wish for?

2. How did Evan's mother help him get his wish?

3. What did Evan do to make his corner look nice?

4. Even after fixing up his corner, Evan wasn't happy. Did Evan understand why he wasn't happy? Who did understand?

5. Have you ever wished for a place of your own? Why or why not?

6. If you had been Evan, what would you have done to fix up your corner?

7. Have you ever helped someone else do something? How did it make you feel?

The Victory

The kids at Joliet are clever all right. By clever, I mean that they know the important things in life. If you tell a Joliet kid a secret, that kid will keep the secret. And you can't just tell a Joliet kid something and expect him or her to believe it. A Joliet kid needs proof. If you try to fake a Joliet kid, you probably won't get away with it. Not all Joliet kids end up at a university, that's true. But in their own way, Joliet kids are very shrewd.

Other schools around the city think they are more clever than we are. That is why we were so happy to be invited to the TV show. You've probably seen the show on your own TV screen. It's the show where they ask kids questions, and one school wins every week. The questioner on the show, Rob Ray, looks like he has a thousand teeth in his mouth. It was the first time our school had been asked to provide a team. We didn't care how long we lasted on the show. We just wanted to beat one other team. For our school, that would be enough of a feat.

The first thing we had to do was choose a team. That was no easy feat, since everyone wanted to be on it. Finally, the whole school decided. In secret, each kid put one name on a piece of paper. The top four winners would go to the TV show. I am happy to say that I was picked to go. Katherine Bailey also was picked for the team. Everyone knows how smart she is. Then George Thomas was picked. And the fourth member was Richard Grant, my best friend. Richard cannot hear. Because of this, he has learned to talk in sign language. Because of our friendship, I have also learned how to use sign language.

The week before the show, we learned that we were playing against Roosevelt, one of the top schools around. As soon as our team heard that, they began to talk in disappointed tones.

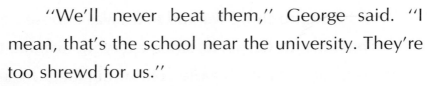

"We'll never beat them," George said. "I mean, that's the school near the university. They're too shrewd for us."

The kids at Roosevelt were shrewd. We didn't need any special proof of that. You can imagine how much we wanted to beat *that* team.

"We forgot something," Richard signed to me.

"What?" I signed.

"The rules should help us," he said with his hands. Richard explained that the rules of the show did not help experts in one subject. The best teams were those who knew about many different subjects. Roosevelt was filled with kids who were experts in one subject only.

There was only one person on our team who was that kind of expert. It was Richard himself. Richard knows a lot about books, science, and math, but he knows nothing about some things. He knows nothing about games like football, because he doesn't enjoy them. At that moment, I'm sure each team member made a secret wish. We wished that any questions about games would go to one of us, and not to Richard.

Richard began signing again. I laughed.

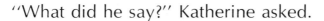

"What did he say?" Katherine asked.

"He said that he hopes the questioner doesn't ask him about games," I said. Then we all laughed.

For the next few weeks, everyone on the team was glued to the television screen when the show came on. At last, the day of the big show arrived.

The building was huge, and all the people made us feel like stars. Of course, we were the stars in a way. A woman showed us where to sit. By signing, I said to Richard, "Your seat, sir." He bowed deeply and sat down. I bent down too low. My head bumped the desk.

291

A man ran over. "Please don't touch anything," he said in an uneasy tone.

Just then the Roosevelt team came in. They hardly looked at us as they took their seats.

Then in came Rob Ray, the real star of the show, the questioner. Suddenly, the lights around the stage went out. Rob Ray pulled out a card and said, "OK, this is for Richard Grant of Joliet."

The question was about the two sources of sugar. The rules of the game said the person asked the question had to provide the answer. As we had planned, I signed the question, and Richard signed the answer. Then I gave Richard's answer for the two sources of sugar.

The Roosevelt team howled. The questioner, Rob Ray, howled. "Stop the show!" he screamed in an angry tone of voice. "You can't provide him with the answer. You're going to make the show look like a fake."

Well, that made *me* angry. "In the first place," I said, "I didn't tell Richard the answer to the question. He told me the two sources of sugar. Richard can't hear. That's all. In the second place, the show won't look like a fake, because it isn't a fake. Anybody will be able to tell the answer came from Richard, not from me."

"Yes, but we have no proof of that," said a kid from Roosevelt.

JUDGE

It looked as if the whole show would end right then. However, a woman from the show stepped forward. She was a member of the university and a judge on the show.

The woman said, "I have been a judge on this show for a long time. I have seen a thousand children on this show. We have never had someone on the show who used sign language. I think it's time we did."

Then, to everyone's surprise, she repeated everything she had said by signing. "You see," she said, "I know that Richard got the answer right, because I can also sign. Until I was eight, I could not hear at all."

Of course, everyone on our team cheered. The Roosevelt team and Rob Ray still didn't look very happy, but what could they do? We began again.

The Roosevelt team answered a question about how the hoof of a horse and the hoof of a deer are different. Then Katherine missed a question about how many dimes you could get for a thousand dollars. Then someone from Roosevelt missed a question about a famous story. The story is about a villager in Mexico. The villager finds a stone that turns out to be worth a lot of money.

Questions and answers flew. We did so well, that the score was tied with one question to go. It was Richard's turn.

Rob Ray asked, "What is the name for the circle formed by players to protect their game plans from being seen?"

We looked at Richard, and our hearts sank. He didn't seem to know it. We suddenly remembered how little he knew about games. Then, while we watched, a slow smile spread across Richard's face. He looked at me and winked. His fingers signed the right answer, and I repeated it. We had won!

Later we had a victory party. I asked Richard a question of my own. "How did you know the answer to that last question? I didn't think you knew anything about games." His answer made me laugh.

He told me that that question was easy. The circle formed by players in football was invented by players who could not hear. They played for a school in Washington, D.C. Since these players used sign language to talk about plays, they had to block the view of the other team. They came up with the idea of a circle to protect their plays from being seen.

THINK ABOUT IT

1. Why was the victory so important to the team from Joliet?
2. How did the Joliet school choose its team?
3. What kind of person do you think the person telling this story is?
4. How would you have felt if you had been on the Roosevelt team?
5. Do you think TV shows like the one in this story have any real value to those watching them?
6. What would be most frightening about being on a television show?

WRITE AND READ
ABOUT IT

———————————————————— ONE

Shadow Song, 10-13

✎ Where could shadows hide? What might they be hiding from? Pretend that shadows have lives of their own. Make up a few shadow-people, and write a story about some of the places where shadows hide. You might also want to explain what shadows do on rainy days.

📖 *Think of Shadows* by Lilian Moore (Atheneum Publishers). These poems and pictures of all kinds of shadows will help you to see their very, special beauty.

📖 *Light: Color and Life for the World* by Frederick C. Huber (David McKay Co., Inc.). This book explains the way your eyes and light work together so you can see. It also tells about the many different kinds of light people have made.

Something Odd at the Ball Park, 14-23

✎When would it be fun to wear a rubber nose, a mask, or a funny moustache? Think of as many good times for hiding your true looks as you can. List each time, and beside it tell why you would do it. Here is one way to begin this strange list.

When	Why
1. at dinner	so my parents will think I'm a guest
2. in front of a mirror	so I'll hardly know myself!

Now add your ideas!

📖 *The Ball Park: One Day Behind the Scenes at a Major League Game* by William Jaspersohn (Little, Brown & Company). The story and photos in this book show how Boston's Fenway Park looks before, during, and after a big game.

📖 *The Diamond Champs* by Matt Christopher (Little, Brown & Company). Tim Rollins is puzzled by the new coach. Read this book to find out why.

The Merry Menagerie, 24-33

✎ What do you think it would be like to be the President's child? Would it be fun for you, or would you like a more private life? Would you like appearing in the newspapers and on TV? When people didn't agree with what your mother or father did, would you be upset? What parts of being the President's child would you like, and what parts would be hard for you? Write about them.

📖 *Theodore Roosevelt* by Sibyl Hancock (G. P. Putnam's Sons). This book tells the life story of President Theodore Roosevelt.

📖 *The Last Cow on the White House Lawn* by Barbara Seuling (Doubleday & Company). There are interesting bits of facts about each President in this book.

📖 *White House Children* by Miriam Anne Bourne (Random House). Little stories tell about family life in the White House.

3-D Pictures, 34-37

✎ Sometimes a painting, a photo, or a TV picture looks so good to you that you wish you could walk right into it. Think about what would happen if you could. Choose a picture and, in your mind, walk into it. What will you do in there? What will you see, feel, hear, and smell? Write about the picture world you visit.

📖 *Three-D, Two-D, One-D* by David A. Adler (Thomas Y. Crowell Company). Two comic explorers and a talking goat help to teach you all about the three dimensions.

The Search for the Mississippi, 38-47

✎ In what ways were Marquette and Joliet like space explorers? In what ways were they different? Make a chart to help you think it through. Write Marquette and Joliet on one side of the page and Space Explorers on the other. Now think about the ways exploring space and exploring the unknown parts of the country are the same and ways in which they are different.

Write things that are the same for both across the whole page. Write the things that are different beside each other. Here's how to begin.

<u>Marquette and Joliet</u>   <u>Space Explorers</u>

They were both taking risks.

They set out on their own.   They have many people on Earth helping them.

📖*Journeys on the Mississippi* by Kay Cooper (Julian Messner). Here are more stories and facts about that great river.

📖*Wilderness Challenge* (National Geographic Society). This is a book about how groups of kids have explored mountains, white water rivers, and other parts of the American wilderness. The book gives guidelines for doing it yourself.

📖*Marquette & Joliet: Voyagers on the Mississippi* by Ronald Syme (William Morrow & Co., Inc.). To find out much more about these daring explorers, read this book.

Los Muchachos, 48-52

✎Think about a world in which people only worked when they felt like working. It sounds great, doesn't it? But what would happen in people's homes, in stores, in schools, on TV and radio, and everywhere else, when people didn't feel like working? What results might that bring? Write about a day when the working world breaks down. Tell what happens.

📖*El Circo Magico Modelo: Finding the Magic Circus* by MacDuff Everton (Carolrhoda Books, Inc.). This is the true story of a trip the writer and his son made to find the circus where the writer once worked.

📖*Born on the Circus* by Fred Powledge (Harcourt Brace Jovanovich, Inc.). Black-and-white photos and a lively story tell about an 11-year-old American boy's life and work in a circus.

📖*Take a Trip to Spain* by Jonathan Rutland (Franklin Watts, Inc.). This easy-to-read book has bright, color photos and tells a bit about Spain.

Company Clothes, 53

✎Write about your favorite old clothes. You may love an old pair of jeans, a worn-out jacket, or some dirty old sneakers. How do your favorite clothes feel special? What do you really like about them? Do you remember any good times you had when you wore those clothes?

📖 *Any Me I Want to Be* by Karla Kuskin (Harper Junior Books). These poems say "I'm me, and I'm one-of-a-kind!"

_____ **TWO**

The Great Wave, 56-67

✎Take some time to watch some water. Look at it as it pours into the tub or sprays out of a sprinkler. Watch rain running down windows or streaming along the sides of city streets. How does water move? Does it spill, spin, or splash? What does it look like? Like ribbons, or tubes, or broken glass?

(Continue on next page.)

What does water sound like? A whisper, a tiny bell tinkling, or like something else? Look and listen carefully. Then write about water.

Angry Waters: Floods and Their Control by R. V. Fodor (Dodd, Mead & Company). This is a book about different kinds of floods, their causes, and what can be done about them.

A Week in Windley's World: Hawaii by Fred Lyon (Crowell-Collier Press). Photos and a story tell about a boy's everyday life in Hawaii.

Make No Sound by Barbara Corcoran (Atheneum Publishers). This book for good readers tells about the difficulties and exciting experiences of a family who moves to Hawaii.

The Crystal Flask, 68-77

If tears and laughter could be bottled, you could fill a jar with wishes! First, think about the most wonderful things that could happen to you. Think about your favorite kinds of days, the people you like best, and the nicest things to do.

Then write each wish you make on its own brightly, colored slip of paper, fold it up, and put it in the jar. As you think of new wishes, write them down, and add them. From time to time, take out a wish, unfold it and read it. Sit back and smile about your good ideas!

The Wishing Bottle by Sheila Dolan (Houghton, Mifflin Company). Nora finds an old bottle, cleans it up, and uses it to wish for a pony.

Have Some Fun, 78-79

Make up a cartoon character. What kinds of things could he or she do to make you smile? Maybe you should give your character a funny name that's a clue to the way he or she will behave. Draw a picture and keep changing your character's looks until he or she is very funny. Then, write some stories about your character.

Ed Emberley's Drawing Book: Make a World by Ed Emberley (Little, Brown & Company). This book teaches you to draw all kinds of things.

The Art of the Comic Strip by Shirley Glubok (Macmillan Publishing Company, Inc.). Here's your chance to see lots of old newspaper comic strips and to find out how comics began in the United States.

A Homemade Television Set, 80-83

Pretend you have a TV talk show of your own. Think about the people you would like to have on the show as guests. Plan your first show. What questions would you ask your guest? What answers do you think your guest would give? Write about the way that first show would run.

What Makes TV Work by Scott Corbett (Little, Brown & Company). This book tells where the pictures on television come from and how they get into your TV set.

Television Magic by Eurfron Gwynne Jones (The Viking Press). Besides telling you how TV works, this book gives things to do that will help you learn firsthand how shows are made.

How Do We Know About Dinosaurs?, 84-93

✎Think about what you know about dinosaurs and the world in which they lived. How do you think they might have spent their days? And at night, while dinosaurs were asleep, what did they dream? Write about a dinosaur dream.

📖*My Visit to the Dinosaurs* by Aliki (T. Y. Crowell & Co.). This book shows how people find, study, save, and put together dinosaur bones.

📖*They Lived With the Dinosaurs* by Russell Freedman (Holiday House). Photos and stories tell about animals that have stayed the same since they lived with dinosaurs.

The Cat Sat on the Mat, 94-102

✎Whoever heard of washing someone and hanging her out to dry! It's a good thing Emma's skin didn't wrinkle and need to be ironed! What might have happened if the colors of her skin and dress ran in the wash water? Write a silly story about a shop that washes and dries people. What kinds of things could happen there?

307

▭*Soonie and the Dragon* by Shirley Rousseau Murphy (Atheneum Publishers). A poor girl sets out to make her way among strange, magical animals.

▭*Clever Gretchen and Other Forgotten Folktales* retold by Alison Lurie (Thomas Y. Crowell Company). In these stories, bright, brave girls save the day over and over again.

Who's In?, 103

✎Have you ever suspected that things moved around when you weren't looking? Did you believe that your toys played together while you were sleeping? As you were about to fall asleep, couldn't you almost feel your bed begin to float? Begin with one of those ideas and make up lots of details to add. Work them all together into a story.

▭*The Dog Writes on the Window With His Nose* by David Kherdian (Four Winds Press). These poems may open your eyes and help you to see things in new ways.

City and Suburb: Exploring an Ecosystem by Laurence Pringle (Macmillan Publishing Company, Inc.). This book tells how plants, animals, and people live together in busy cities.

Secret Neighbors: Wildlife in a City Lot by Mary Adrian (Hastings House Publishers). The stories of bees, alley cats, spiders, mice, and other things come alive in this book.

THREE

The Story Teller, 106-115

Would you like to star in a movie? Think about the best movies you have seen. Which ones might have been fun for the actors? Write about the kind of part you would like to play and the things you might do if you were a movie star.

Marv by Marilyn Sachs (Doubleday & Company, Inc.). Frances Green calls her younger brother, Marv, a dreamer. She thinks he wastes his time dreaming up all kinds of funny machines. But Marv proves she is wrong.

Ellen Grae by Vera and Bill Cleaver (J. B. Lippincott Company). Away from her family for the school year, Ellen Grae learns a hard lesson about telling the truth.

Finding Your Way, 116-117

Do you ever lose your way? How do you feel then? What different things can you do to help find the direction you need to go? Are there things you can do to make yourself feel better when you're lost? Think about these questions and answer them as you write.

A Map Is a Picture by Barbara Rinkoff (Thomas Y. Crowell). In this book, you'll find a quick look at many different kinds of maps.

Train Ride to Freedom, 118-127

Think about someone you know well. Pick a person you think is special. Then, think about his or her character. What does that person say and do that is important to you? What do you like about that person? Write as much as you can.

📖 *Frederick Douglass: Boy Champion of Human Rights* by Elisabeth P. Myers (Bobbs-Merrill Co., Inc.). The story of this brave, thoughtful man's life is told in this book.

📖 *When the Rattlesnake Sounds* by Alice Childress (Coward, McCann & Geoghegan, Inc.). This is a play about one summer in Harriet Tubman's life.

There Isn't Time, 128-129

✎ List ten things you would like to do during your lifetime. If you can't think of ten, list as many as you can. Study your list and then put the things in order. Make number one the most important thing on your list. Make number ten the least important. After you've done that, ask yourself, "What did I find out about me?" Think about your list. Then write about your discoveries.

📖 *Small Wonders* by Norma Farber (Coward, McCann & Geoghegan, Inc.). These poems point out the things you might miss on a busy day.

String Things, 130-133

✎Write a recipe that tells how to make a friendship. First, list all the things someone might need. Don't forget to tell how much of each thing to use. Then add some directions for putting everything together. If you need to, look at cookbook recipes for ideas. Write your recipe on a card and decorate it if you like.

📖 *Beginning Mobiles* by Peggy Parish (Macmillan Publishing Co.). This book tells how to make all kinds of hanging things out of string, straws, and other easy-to-find objects.

The World's Best-Known Lamb, 134-139

✎Change the color of Mary's little lamb in the poem and add two new lines of your own. Here are some colors to try: bright as gold, dirty brown, very black, dark as night, almost pink, and nearly blue. First, think of some words that rhyme with a color word. Then, try to make the new lines have the same beat as the old ones. What do the rhyming words lead you to say in the poem?

📖*Lambs for Dinner* by Betsy Maestro (Crown Publishers, Inc.). This is an old story with a new twist.

📖*A Nursery Companion* edited by Iona and Peter Opie (Oxford University Press). Rhymes you will remember and some you never heard before are printed with wonderful artwork from old books.

Heat Wave, 140-149

✏️In the story you just read, the writer played with ideas and sounds. Remember the king who was "roasting in his royal robes"? Use some other cooking words in sentences in which most of the words begin with the same or nearly the same sound. Here's how.

> A <u>t</u>ired <u>t</u>ourist <u>t</u>oasted in a <u>t</u>errible <u>t</u>own.
> <u>B</u>ailey <u>b</u>aked under a <u>b</u>undle of <u>b</u>ibs.

Try making up your own sentences using *mixed, tossed, boiled, froze,* and *cooked.* Think of as many words as you can that start with the same sound as each cooking word. Then, build the longest sentences you can with them!

313

📖 *The Blue Moose* by Manus Pinkwater (Dodd, Mead & Co.). A friendly moose comes to work in a restaurant and tries to cheer up its owner and cook.

📖 *Wanda and the Bumbly Wizard* by James Flora (Atheneum Publishers). Wanda meets a wizard who makes one terrible error after another in this very funny picture book.

FOUR

Laughing Time, 152-153

✎ Make up a very short, funny story in which you rhyme as many words as you can. First find a group of many words that end with the same sounds. (Here's a hint. You already know lots of words that rhyme with *fly, day, old, line, bright,* or *nest.*) Search through the words in your head until you find a group of rhyming ones you like. The rhymes will tell you what your story will have to be about. What you write will probably be strange and silly!

Poetry for Chuckles and Grins edited by Leland B. Jacobs (Garrard Publishing Co.). Poems to play with and laugh about are in this book.

Laughing Time by William Jay Smith (Delacorte Press). The man who wrote the poem in your book wrote still other playful poems you can enjoy.

Masks, 154-157

If there were a magic mask you could put on so that no one could see you, what would you do? Where would you go? When would you wear the mask? Make up a story about using the mask to help you be in all sorts of interesting places.

Mask Magic by Carolyn Meyer (Harcourt Brace Jovanovich). This book tells how you can make and have fun with all kinds of masks.

Word of Mouth, 158-163

If we still got our news from town criers the news might start, "It's six o'clock. All is well!"

(Continue on next page.)

What news would a town crier call out tonight? You may want to have the crier give only school or neighborhood news. Make the news funny or serious, as you please. Write it, then sing it out for some friends.

📖 *Face Talk, Hand Talk, Body Talk* by Sue Castle (Doubleday & Company). Mostly photos, this book shows how much we say without words.

📖 *Slanguage: America's Second Language* by Gibson Carothers and James Lacey (Sterling Publishing Company, Inc.). This book is like HELP WITH WORDS at the back of this book, but it explains many of the funny spoken phrases that color our language.

The One in the Middle Is the Green Kangaroo, 164-171

✎ If you were in a play and had to look like a fish, what would you wear? What would you put on to look like a beaver or a TV? Think about all the things you could use to make the costumes. Then write about how you would do it.

📖 *A Surprise for Carlotta* by Nellie Burchardt (Franklin Watts). Carlotta feels left out of things at school and at home.

📖 *Ellen and the Gang* by Frieda Friedman (William Morrow & Co., Inc.). After some hard times Ellen, a middle child, finds her place among friends and in her neighborhood.

Danger, 172-181

✎ Think of some colorful language you can use to write about the following actions.

getting out of bed	climbing stairs
eating something	riding a bus
walking outside	talking with a friend

Here's one way to write about getting up. I started out of bed like a fire fighter answering an alarm. Make up your own way, now. Write each action in a way that shows how you feel about it.

📖 *Janet Reachfar and Chickabird* by Jane Duncan (Seabury Press). A little girl on a farm in Scotland saves a chick that has been badly hurt.

One for the Computo, 182-191

✎ Think about some ways you could earn money at a school fair. You could paint faces or sell chances on a surprise box lunch. You can probably think of other things to do as well. Sort out your ideas. Then, write about what you would do.

📖 *What Can She Be? A Computer Scientist* by Gloria and Esther Goldreich (Lothrop, Lee & Shepard Co.). This book tells how some people work with computers.

📖 *Miss Pickerell Meets Mr. H.U.M.* by Ellen MacGregor and Dora Pantell (McGraw-Hill Book Company). Miss Pickerell fights back when she discovers a giant computer that wants to take over the world.

Follow Along, 192-193

✎ Make up some riddles. First decide where your riddle clues will lead. Choose an answer (paint, a duck, or something else!) before you make up the questions. Think up clues that are a bit confusing. Here's a riddle question.

What kind of coat can a building wear?

(a coat of paint)

Test the riddles you make up on your friends. They can tell if they're too hard or too easy. Make up a book of brand-new riddles.

📖 *Riddles, Riddles Everywhere* by Ennis Rees (Abelard-Schulman Ltd.) and *Riddle Riot* by Mike Thaler (Scholastic Inc.). If you are a riddle fan, here are two books full of both famous and new riddles.

_____ **FIVE**

The Tale of the Lazy Donkey, 196-205

✏️ Do you believe the old saying, "Sticks and stones may break my bones, but names will never hurt me?" If not, why not? If so, explain why. Write about what you think.

📖 *Once in a Wood: Ten Tales from Aesop* retold by Eve Rice (Greenwillow Books). Here are some good old tales about learning.

Bread Clay, 206-209

✎ Bread that people can't eat is a kind of opposite. Here are some others.

cold fire	a tall valley
clear fog	inside out
sad joy	a short giant
hot ice	pretty ugly

Read the opposites above a few times to get you thinking. Then choose one, and use it as the main idea in a poem or description. Choose colorful language to bring out how strange and interesting the opposite is. Let the opposites pull your mind in two directions at once as you write.

📖 *Bake Bread* by Hannah Solomon (J. B. Lippincott & Co.). With this book, you will be able to bake good-tasting bread.

📖 *Clay Dough, Play Dough* by Goldie T. Chernoff (Walker & Company). Here are some more things to do with salt flour dough.

The Fastest Car in the World, 210-219

✎ Pretend you are the very first person in America to ride a bike or to roller skate. You try out this exciting new toy on a smooth city street. Before long, a curious crowd has gathered. Suddenly, everyone is looking at you!

The next morning, you rush to your office at the newspaper and write the story. Tell the world what you did and how you felt gliding along, powered by your own muscles. At the end of your story, you may even want to hint that bikes or roller skates might one day become important!

📖 *The Flying Machine: A Stage Coach Journey in 1774* by John J. Loeper (Atheneum Publishers). Travel between Philadelphia and New York City was truly exciting in the days just before the American Revolution.

📖 *The Railroads* by Leonard Everett Fisher (Holiday House). This book tells all about the early railroads and how they grew.

Popcorn, 220-226

✎Think about a friend who goes back a long way. How long have you known him or her? What do you like about each other? Would you go out of your way for this friend? Why or why not? Write about this old friend.

📖 *What Makes Popcorn Pop?* by Dave Woodside (Atheneum Publishers). The history of popcorn, some good ideas for enjoying it, and some very odd facts about it are all here in this book.

📖 *Cornzapoppin! Popcorn Recipes & Party Ideas for All Occasions* by Barbara Williams (Holt, Rinehart & Winston). Clear directions for things to make for every month are in this calendar book.

Basketball and Bells, 227-237

✎ Maria Sanchez delivers her papers at dawn. Have you ever seen dawn's special light and felt its quiet? Think of its sights, sounds, smells, and special feelings. Pick words that help describe that time of day clearly. Then write about it.

📖 *Wendy and the Bullies* by Nancy K. Robinson (Hastings House Publishers). Wendy makes a careful study of the bullies in her neighborhood and decides what to do about them.

Keep Track, 238-239

✏️ Graphs can help you remember certain kinds of things, and writing can help you remember other things. Some people keep a book to write in every day. This kind of book is called a *journal.*

Look back over last week. What happened that you especially enjoyed? Save the experience by writing about it. Choose the best words you can to describe each part of the experience. Tell about sights, sounds, feelings, and even tastes.

My Dog Is a Plumber, 240-241

✏️ You have just been named The Most Perfect Girl or The Most Perfect Boy in America. You're about to walk on stage to receive the prize. Why did the judges decide to give it to you? What makes you the special one? Write a speech you will give to explain why the judges were right!

📖*By George, Bloomers!* by Judith St. George (Coward, McCann & Geoghegan, Inc.). A short, easy-to-read story about a time when very few women dared to wear long pants.

📖*Rupert Piper and the Boy Who Could Knit* by Ethelyn Parkinson (Abingdon Press). A story about some people who get upset with a boy who does what he likes.

SIX _____

Use Your Head, Tom 244-255

✏️ Tom Bluewater wants to be an artist. Is that a good thing to be? Why or why not? What do you think is the best work a person could do? Write what you think and explain why you think the way you do.

📖*Special Friends* by Terry Berger (Julian Messner). Photos and an easy-to-read story tell about the friendship of a young girl and the old woman who lives next door.

Open the Door and See All the People by Clyde Robert Bulla (Thomas Y. Crowell Company). After a fire burns everything they own, Joanne, Teeney, and their mother move to the city and learn some new values.

Su Ling's Arrow, 256-267

The writer of "Su Ling's Arrow" said that the river became meaner and meaner. The river is described as if it were a person, with a person's feelings and actions.

Think about the night. Can you describe it as if it were a person? Would it be male or female? Young or old? What kind of clothes would it wear? What would it do? Here is one way to describe night as a person: *Night slid through the sky on skates. She wore glitter in her hair.*

Think about *morning,* or *joy,* or *peace* as if each one was a person. Write a few descriptions for each one. Then pick the best ones and copy them. They are probably the ones that make the clearest and liveliest pictures in your mind.

The Terrible Nung Gwama retold by Ed Young (Collins-World, Inc.). This is a very, exciting Chinese folktale.

The White Archer: An Eskimo Legend by James Houston (Harcourt Brace Jovanovich, Inc.). When he loses his parents and sister, young Kungo decides to become a great archer. When at last he has a chance to get even with his enemies, Kungo finds a better way to teach them a lesson.

Professor Coconut and the Thief, 268-277

Tall tales make everything bigger and better or worse! Make up a character who is even more forgetful than Professor Coconut. What might he or she do that shows how terribly forgetful someone might be! Here are some ideas you might use.

The person could—
1. go to the wrong house and not notice the wrong family was there!
2. forget to go to sleep.
3. forget words for things.
4. forget to walk.

Try out these or your own ideas as you work on a story. If your character jumps, let him or her hop over the clouds. Push your descriptions as far as they will go!

📖 *Mystery of Bleeker Street* by William H. Hooks (Alfred A. Knopf). Ten-year-old Chase and his 78-year-old friend, Babette, get into trouble in New York City and discover a mystery.

Cut-Ups, 278-280

✎ Look around you. Make a list of all the things that you find with squares or triangles on them. They can be square or triangle shaped, too. Keep two different lists so you don't get confused. Work on the lists for a few weeks. Are there more triangles or more squares in the world?

📖 *The Neat Stuff Something-To-Do Book* by Thomas F. Ris (Julian Messner). Here are all sorts of good things to do and make.

Evan's Corner, 281-287

✎ If you could have any room in the world for yourself, what would it be like? Would it have plants and pictures like Evan's corner? In what way would it be special? Think, draw a picture, and write about the room you would like.

📖 *Gabrielle & Selena* by Peter Desbarats (Coward, McCann & Geoghegan). Two girls switch families for a night and find that their own homes and their places in them are special.

The Victory, 288-296

✎ Find some questions and answers that could be used on a TV show like the one in the story. You can get facts from newspapers, magazines, or books. Be sure to write both the question and answer for each fact. Make up teams of your friends and try out your questions.

📖 *Meaning Well* by Sheila R. Cole (Franklin Watts, Inc.). Peggy has a hard time with people in her class because she is a little different.

HELP WITH WORDS

How to Use HELP WITH WORDS

HELP WITH WORDS was written to help you understand certain words found in the stories and articles in this book. It is shorter than a full dictionary. However, it has many of the helps you will find in other dictionaries.

Alphabetical Order

The words that begin with **a** come first in HELP WITH WORDS. Those that begin with **b** come next, and so on. You may need to check beyond the first letter of the word you want if another word begins with the same letter or letters. For example, in these word pairs, which word comes first in the dictionary:

1. **accident** or **adobe?**
2. **colt** or **conductor?**
3. **pause** or **passenger?**
4. **caption** or **capture?**

Guide Words

Look at the words **bray** and **conductor** at the top of page 334. These two words are called "guide words" because they help you find the word you want. The left guide word on each page is the same as the first word explained on that page. The right guide word is the same as the last word explained on that page.

Entry Words

Find the word **accident** on page 333. Notice that it is printed in heavy black type. Such a word is called an "entry word." HELP WITH WORDS does not list entry words for names of people and places. It does list prefixes like **mis-** and suffixes like **-ist.**

Help with Spelling and Writing

Here is the entry for **accident.**

> **ac·ci·dent** (ak′sə dənt)
> something that happens
> by chance

How is **accident** spelled? In HELP WITH WORDS, the centered dots show where you may break a word at the end of a line in writing. After what letters may you break the word **accident**?

All dictionaries give you help with forms of words if there is a spelling change before **-ed, -ing, -er, -est, -s,** or **-es.** Note the entry word **bore** on page 333. Why do the forms **bored** and **boring** also appear?

Help with Meanings

A full dictionary gives all the meanings for a word. HELP WITH WORDS gives the meaning of the word as it is used in your book. For some words, it also gives other common meanings. The different meanings of a word are numbered so that you can find them quickly.

For help in understanding meanings, example sentences are sometimes given. For some entry words, pictures are used to help explain the meaning. A blue dot (•) appears after the meaning for each word that is pictured.

Help with Pronunciation

The pronunciation is given right after the entry word:

ac·ci·dent (ak′sə dənt)

The symbols after the entry word show how the word **accident** is pronounced or spoken. These symbols sometimes look a lot like the entry word:

dusk (dusk)

Often, however, they look different:

ex·claim (ek sklām′)

When there is more than one way to pronounce a word, HELP WITH WORDS shows the pronunciations this way:

ei·ther (ē′ŦHər *or* ī′ŦHər)

Look once again at the pronunciation symbols for **exclaim**:

ex·claim (ek sklām′)

Notice that (sklām′) is followed by a heavy mark called a "stress mark." This shows which part of the word **exclaim** is stressed, or said more loudly. In some words a second stress mark is shown this way: (fer′ē bōt′)

All of the pronunciation symbols used in HELP WITH WORDS are shown on the next page. Some of these symbols are also shown in the key at the bottom of every right-hand page.

Study the symbols on page 332 carefully. Some look just like the letters of the alphabet: /a/. Others have marks that make them look different from letters: /ā/. The important thing to remember about both kinds of symbols is that they do not stand for letters; they stand for sounds.

Pronunciation Symbols

a	as, cat	o	not
ā	lady, take, rain, play, weight	ō	open, no, hope, show, road, four
ä	father, borrow, car	ô	toss, ought, ball, fault, saw, caught
		oi	point, boy
b	bib, robber	ou	loud, town
ch	church, catch, picture, question		
d	dad, sadder	p	paper, happy, up
		r	roar, hurry, write, rhyme
e	let, head, care	s	sat, yes, class, city, nice, scene, mouse
ē	me, need, seat, these, happy, radio, monkey, movie, equal	sh	shop, dash, station, special, expression, patient
ėr	hurt, learn, her, bird, work, term	t	tight, better
f	fit, if, off, phone, laugh	th	thing, teeth
g	got, buggy, guess, ghost	ŦH	this, smooth
h	hit, behind, who		
		u	rug, touch, son, done
i	sit, gym, enough	u̇	put, book, could
ī	like, try, kind, pie, bright	ü	truth, rule, move, soon, blue, new, to
j	jet, gem, edge, cage		
k	kick, cap, mechanic	v	vet, have
l	like, color, until, fall	w	win, away
m	mom, summer, climb	y	you, yet
n	noon, manner, know, gnaw	z	zoo, puzzle, rose, was
ng	ring, thing	zh	vision, treasure

ə
{
a in about, probably, dollar
e in belong, majesty, open
i in giraffe, president, cabin
o in compare, violin, wagon
u in suppose, instrument, circus
}

Aa

ac•ci•dent (ak'sə dənt) something that happens by chance

a • do • be (ə dō' bē) **1** brick made of sun-dried earth and straw **2** a building made of adobe bricks ●

age•less (āj'lis) never growing old or showing the effects of age

aim (ām) to point to or toward something (Don't *aim* the hose at me.)

alike (ə līk') like one another; in the same manner

ar • e • a (er'ē ə *or* ar'ē ə) a level piece of ground; a flat space

art•ist (är'tist) a person skilled in one of the arts, such as painting, music, or writing, especially a painter ●

au•di•ence (ô'dē əns) a group of people gathered in one place to listen to or watch something (The *audience* clapped when the guest speaker walked on stage.)

adobe

Bb

bal•ance (bal'əns) **bal•anced; bal•anc•ing** to hold steady

barbed wire (bärbd wīr) twisted wires with sharp points used to make fences ●

bil•low (bil'ō) to rise or swell in big waves (Smoke *billowed* from the chimney.)

bore (bôr *or* bōr) **bored; bor•ing** to tire by being dull (This game *bores* me.)

artist

a	hat	ō	open	sh	she
ā	age	ô	order	th	thin
ä	far	oi	oil	ŦH	then
e	let	ou	out	zh	measure
ē	equal	u	cup		a in about
ėr	term	ù	put		e in taken
i	it	ü	rule	ə =	i in pencil
ī	ice	ch	child		o in lemon
o	hot	ng	long		u in circus

barbed wire

burro

canoe

conductor

bray (brā) a loud crying sound of a burro or other pack animal

broth·er·hood (bruŦH'ər hùd) the state of being brothers; as, joined in *brotherhood*

buf·fa·lo (buf'ə lō) **buf·fa·loes** a wild American ox

bulk · y (bul' kē) **bulk·i·er; bulk·i·est** being large and hard to hold (The *bulky* box would not fit into the car.)

bur·ro (bėr'ō *or* bùr'ō) a small horselike animal used for riding or carrying things

Cc

ca·noe (kə nü') a narrow, lightweight boat that has curved sides and pointed ends and is moved by paddles

cap·tion (kap'shən) a group of words used to explain a picture

cap·ture (kap'chər) **cap·tured; cap·tur·ing** to take over something or someone by force (The soldiers *captured* the enemy.)

car·ni·val (kär'nə vəl) a place set up with rides and games

ce·re·al (sir'ē əl) a food made from grain

chunk (chungk) a short, thick piece or lump

clev·er (klev'ər) **1** bright; smart **2** showing skill

cliff (klif) a high, steep rockface (We watched as two women climbed the *cliff.*)

colt (kōlt) a young horse

con·duc·tor (kən duk'tər) **1** a person in charge of collecting tickets on a train **2** the leader of a music group

334

cre·ate (krē āt′) **cre·at·ed; cre·at·ing** to make or form (I *created* this design by using a triangle.)

croak (krōk) a low, rough sound (Frogs and crows *croak.*)

crow (krō) a shiny black bird that has a loud cry ●

crum·ble (krum′bəl) **crum·bled; crum·bling** to break into small pieces; to fall into pieces (The dry earth *crumbled* in their hands.)

crys·tal (kris′tl) a clear glass having no color ●

cu·ri·ous (kyùr′ē əs) wanting to know something; eager to learn (Aren't you *curious* about how the story ends?)

cur·tain (kėrt′n) a piece of cloth meant to darken, hide, or decorate (We bought new *curtains* for my bedroom windows.)

Dd

dain·ti·ly (dān′tə lē) in a soft, pleasing way

dark·en (där′kən) to make or grow dark or darker

dawn (dôn) early morning

deal (dēl) a measure not fixed or limited (His act caused a great *deal* of laughter.)

de·scribe (di skrīb′) **de·scribed; de·scrib·ing** to tell about something in detail (Can you *describe* the jacket he's wearing?)

de·scrip·tion (di skrip′shən) a word picture of someone or something (The police have a *description* of my bike.)

crow

crystal

a	hat	ō	open	sh	she
ā	age	ô	order	th	thin
ä	far	oi	oil	ŦH	then
e	let	ou	out	zh	measure
ē	equal	u̇	cup		a in about
ėr	term	ù	put		e in taken
i	it	ü	rule	ə =	i in pencil
ī	ice	ch	child		o in lemon
o	hot	ng	long		u in circus

335

diner

dinosaur

di·a·gram (dī′ə gram) a drawing or sketch that makes something clearer or easier to understand

dime (dīm) a piece of money with a value of ten cents

din·er (dī′nər) a railroad dining car or a restaurant in the shape of one ●

di·no·saur (dī′nə sôr) a member of a group of huge animals that lived on the earth long, long ago ●

dis·ap·pear (dis′ə pir′) to go out of sight; to become lost

dis·cov·ery (dis kuv′ər ē) **dis·cov·er·ies** a new thing seen, learned of, or found

dusk (dusk) the time of evening just before dark (We turn on our lights after *dusk.*)

Ee

earth·en (ėr′thən) made of earth (The pueblo had an *earthen* floor.)

ei·ther (ē′ᴛʜər *or* ī′ᴛʜər) the one or the other; any one of two (*Either* Liz or her brother delivers our newspaper.)

e·nor·mous (i nôr′məs) very large; huge (A bear seems *enormous* next to an ant.)

erase (i rās′) **erased; eras·ing** to rub out or scratch out (She *erased* her error and wrote in the right answer.)

ex·claim (ek sklām′) to cry out or say something suddenly with great feeling

ex·pen·sive (ek spen′siv) very high-priced (The silver necklace was too *expensive* for me to buy.)

ex·plor·er (ek splôr′ər *or* ek splōr′ər) one who hopes to make discoveries; one who searches (Marquette and Joliet were *explorers.*)

Ff

fair·y (fer′ē *or* far′ē) a make-believe being who has magical powers

fake (fāk) **1** false (a *fake* jewel) **2** a person or thing that is not what it is supposed to be (We could see that the jewel was a *fake.*)

fare·well (fer′wel′ *or* far′wel′) a way of saying good-by or parting (She said *farewell* as she left for a vacation.)

fa·vor·ite (fā′vər it) liked best (Chocolate is my *favorite* kind of icing on a cake.)

fer·ry·boat (fer′ē bōt′) a boat that carries people, cars, and goods across a river ●

fig·ure (fig′yər) **fig·ured; fig·ur·ing** **1** to think out in one's head (*figure* out the answer) **2** the shape or form of something

flask (flask) a bottle with a narrow neck ●

fleece (flēs) the coat of wool that covers a sheep

foil (foil) a thin sheet of metal (I wrapped my lunch in a piece of *foil.*)

fos·sil (fos′əl) a trace of a plant or an animal that lived in the past

free·dom (frē′dəm) being free and able to move about or do as one pleases

frown (froun) to wrinkle the face in an angry, unhappy, or disappointed way (Billy *frowned* when I wouldn't let him use my mitt.) ●

ferryboat

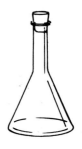

flask

frown

a	hat	ō	open	sh	she
ā	age	ô	order	th	thin
ä	far	oi	oil	ŦH	then
e	let	ou	out	zh	measure
ē	equal	u	cup		⌈ a in about
ėr	term	ù	put		⌈ e in taken
i	it	ü	rule	ə = ⟨ i in pencil
ī	ice	ch	child		⌊ o in lemon
o	hot	ng	long		⌊ u in circus

Gg

gal·lop (gal′əp)   to run at full speed (The horse *galloped* down the road.)

gaze (gāz)   **gazed; gaz·ing**   to fix the eyes in a long and steady look; to stare (Sue *gazed* at the beautiful red sunset.)

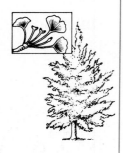

ginkgo

gink·go (ging′kō *or* jing′kō)   **gink·goes** a large Chinese tree with yellow fruit ●

glance (glans)   **glanced; glanc·ing** to give a quick look (I *glanced* at the snapshots.)

glit·ter (glit′ər)   to gleam or shine

greet (grēt)   to speak to in a friendly way; to welcome (They *greeted* us at the front door.)

harness

guf·faw (gu fô′)   a loud kind of laughter (She let out a *guffaw* when she saw the cartoon.)

guin·ea pig (gin′ē pig) a small mammal with sharp front teeth, short ears, and a very short tail

Hh

hard·ship (härd′ship) something that is hard to bear (The storm caused much *hardship.*)

har·ness (här′nis) the leather fastenings placed about the head or body of an animal to control it ●

-hood   a suffix that means **1** a state of being (*childhood*) **2** having or sharing a special character (*brotherhood*)

hoof (hùf *or* hüf) **hooves** *or* **hoofs**   a covering of horn that protects the toes of some animals

hush (hush)   to make or become quiet

Ii

i·mag·ine (i maj′ ən)
i·mag·ined;
i·mag·in·ing to make up an idea or form pictures in the mind ●

in·vent (in vent′) to think up or make up for the first time

in·volve (in volv′)
in·volved;
in·volv·ing to draw into or take part in something (He was *involved* in planning the trip.)

-ist a suffix meaning "one who does or makes something" (*artist*)

Jj

jade (jād) a green stone used in jewelry

jin·gle (jing′gəl)
jin·gled; jin·gling to make a light sound, like that of little bells

jour·ney (jėr′ nē) a trip (Our *journey* lasted six weeks.)

Kk

knee (nē) the place where the lower leg and upper leg come together

Ll

la·va (lä′və *or* lav′ə) melted rock that comes from a volcano

length (lengkth *or* length) how long something is from end to end (The *length* of the bed is six feet.)

-less a suffix meaning "not having something" (*pointless*)

Mm

mar·ket (mär′kit) a place where goods are sold (fruit *market*)

imagine

a	hat	ō	open	sh	she
ā	age	ô	order	th	thin
ä	far	oi	oil	ᴛʜ	then
e	let	ou	out	zh	measure
ē	equal	u	cup		
ėr	term	ù	put		
i	it	ü	rule		
ī	ice	ch	child		
o	hot	ng	long		

ə = a in about, e in taken, i in pencil, o in lemon, u in circus

mare (mer *or* mar) an adult female horse or other horse-like animal (My dad entered his *mare* in the horse show to be held next week.)

me·chan·ic (mə kan′ik) one who makes or fixes cars and machines (The *mechanic* fixed our car.)•

mem·ber (mem′bər) one of the people or units that makes up a group (Billy is a *member* of the school swim team.)

me·nag·er·ie (mə naj′ər ē *or* mə nazh′ər ē) many animals kept together in one place (We have a *menagerie* of pets.)

mis- a prefix meaning "in a bad or wrong way" (*misjudge*)

mist (mist) a cloud of fine rain; haze

mix·ture (miks′chər) different things put together (We drank a *mixture* of lemonade and orangeade.)

mechanic

mus·cle (mus′əl) a part of the body that causes motion and is sometimes attached to bones (After Benny ran the race, his leg *muscles* hurt him.)

mutt (mut) a dog of no certain class or kind (That *mutt* looks like a terrier mix.)

mys·tery (mis′tər ē) **m y s · t e r · i e s** something that has not been explained or that is hard to understand (What the weather will be tomorrow is a *mystery* to me.)

Nn

nei·ther (nē′ᴛHər *or* nī′ᴛHər) not the one and not the other; not either (*Neither* of the two boys wanted to walk the dog.)

-ness a suffix meaning "state of being or feeling" (*sadness*)

nib·ble (nib′əl)
nib·bled; nib·bling
to bite or chew gently •

nick·name (nik′nām′)
nick·named;
nick·nam·ing **1** to
give another name to
someone or something
which describes that
person or thing (They
nicknamed me Curly.)
2 a name used instead
of a person or thing's real
name (Elizabeth's
nickname is Betty.)

non·sense (non′sens)
foolish talk or things that
have no meaning (Do you
know any *nonsense*
rhymes?)

nurse (nèrs) **1** a
person hired for the care
of a young child (The
nurse fed the baby.) **2** a
person skilled or trained
in the care of the sick •

Oo

ob·vi·ous (ob′vē əs)
easy to find, see, or
understand (It was
obvious that Jim was
unhappy.)

oc·ca·sion (ə kā′zhən)
a special time (His
birthday party was a
great *occasion.*)

Pp

pas·sen·ger (pas′n jər)
a person who rides a bus,
train, plane, or other
means of travel

pause (pôz) **paused;**
paus·ing to stop for
a while; wait (He *paused*
when he heard the
whistle.) •

pe·so (pā′sō) **pe·sos**
an old silver coin of Spain

pet·ri·fy (pet′rə fī)
pet·ri·fied;
pet·ri·fy·ing to
change plant or animal
matter into stone
(*petrified* trees)

nibble

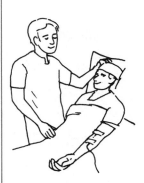

nurse

pause

a	hat	ō	open	sh	she
ā	age	ô	order	th	thin
ä	far	oi	oil	₮H	then
e	let	ou	out	zh	measure
ē	equal	u	cup		a in about
èr	term	ù	put		e in taken
i	it	ü	rule	ə =	i in pencil
ī	ice	ch	child		o in lemon
o	hot	ng	long		u in circus

plen·ti·ful (plen'ti fəl) in great supply (Buffalo were once *plentiful* on the prairies.)

plumb·er (plum'ər) a person who fixes pipes through which water flows (The *plumber* is fixing some pipes in the cellar.)●

plumber

poke (pōk) **poked; pok·ing** 1 to push out or into (He *poked* his nose into our business.) 2 to push against with something pointed (She *poked* me in the arm with her finger.)

pole (pōl) a long, thin piece of wood or metal (The girl on the high wire carried a *pole*.)

prac·tice (prak'tis) **prac·ticed; prac·tic·ing** to do something often so as to learn it or become better at it (Jill *practices* on her flute every afternoon.)

prob·lem (prob'ləm) something that is hard to understand or work out

rein

pro·fes·sor (prəfes'ər) a teacher at a university

pure (pyùr) **pur·er; pur·est** not mixed with anything else (*pure* water)

Qq

ques·tion·er (kwes'chən ər) one who asks questions

Rr

re·cite (ri sīt') **re·cit·ed; re·cit·ing** to repeat from what has been learned or remembered (Can you *recite* any part of the poem you read last week?)

rein (rān) a line or strip leading to an animal's mouth and used to guide it (She pulled on the *reins* to make the horse turn.)●

re·move (ri müv′) **re·moved; re·mov·ing** to move by lifting or taking off (First, *remove* the top from the box.)●

re·triev·er (ri trē′vər) a dog trained to find a dead animal and bring it to the hunter

rid·dle (rid′l) a puzzling question that is answered by guessing (I couldn't guess the answer to the *riddle.*)

risk (risk) to take a chance by doing something filled with danger

roam (rōm) to go from place to place with no certain direction (Dinosaurs *roamed* the earth long, long ago.)

Ss

sad·ness (sad′nis) being sad (It was with *sadness* that we said good-by.)

safe·ly (sāf′lē) free from harm or danger (We made it *safely* home before dark.)

sauce (sôs) a soft mixture served with food to make it taste better (butter *sauce*)

scowl (skoul) to look angry; to frown

screen (skrēn) a curtain used to hide, protect, or keep apart one thing from another (The dining area is set off by a *screen*.)●

se·cret (sē′krit) hidden from others (The old house has a *secret* stairway.)

se·cure (si kyur′) **1** safe from harm (a *secure* country) **2** free from fear or worry (We feel *secure* in our new home.) **3** safely tied (a *secure* rope)

remove

screen

a	hat	ō	open	sh	she
ā	age	ô	order	th	thin
ä	far	oi	oil	ŦH	then
e	let	ou	out	zh	measure
ē	equal	u	cup		a in about
ėr	term	ù	put		e in taken
i	it	ü	rule	ə =	i in pencil
ī	ice	ch	child		o in lemon
o	hot	ng	long		u in circus

shaggy

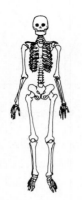

skeleton

speech

seek (sēk) **sought; seek·ing** trying to find, reach, or get something

shag·gy (shag′ē) covered with long, thick hair, wool, or other matter (That *shaggy* dog looks like a dust mop.) ●

-ship a suffix meaning "state of being" (*hardship; friendship*)

skel·e·ton (skel′ə tən) the bones of a person or animal fitted together so as to show the body form (Scientists have dug up *skeletons* of animals believed to have lived millions of years ago.) ●

slit (slit) a long and narrow cut or opening (The rain came in through a *slit* in the side of the tent.)

snort (snôrt) to make a loud, rough sound by pushing air through the nose (The horse *snorted* and frightened us.)

sol·id (sol′id) being the same thing throughout (a *solid* green coat)

sort (sôrt) a group of things of the same kind or type (What *sort* of cake is that?)

source (sôrs *or* sōrs) the place from which something comes (What is the *source* of your information?)

sped (sped) a past form of *speed* meaning "moved quickly; hurried" (The fire fighters *sped* to the rescue.)

speech (spēch) a public talk (The explorer gave a *speech* on her discovery.) ●

star·tle (stär′tl) **star·tled; star·tling** to cause to jump suddenly in surprise or fear (The thunder *startled* me so that I dropped my book.)

state (stāt) one of the units that are joined to form the United States (Many slaves ran away to the northern *states*.)

streak (strēk) a line of a different color from its background (His red shirt has large yellow *streaks* down the side.)

strug·gle (strug′əl) **strug·gled; strug·gling** to try against great odds (The swimmer *struggled* against the tide.)

sub·sti·tute (sub′stə tüt *or* sub′stə tyüt) **sub·sti·tut·ed; sub·sti·tut·ing** to use or take in place of another thing or person (Fay *substituted* for her brother in the game.)

swamp (swomp *or* swômp) muddy land that is partly covered by water (Do any animals live in the *swamp*?)

swift (swift) moving at a very fast speed (To win the race, she had to be very *swift*.)

swirl (swėrl) to move in a twisting course (The water was *swirling* in the washing machine.) ●

swish (swish) to move with a light swinging motion (The donkey *swished* its tail.)

Tt

tale (tāl) a story about happenings that are often made up (She read a *tale* about ghosts.)

tea·ket·tle (tē′ket′l) a covered pot used to boil water

test (test) to try out (Let's *test* the mixture.)

thou·sand (thou′znd) a very large number (Almost a *thousand* people came to the fair.)

swirl

a	hat	ō	open	sh	she	
ā	age	ô	order	th	thin	
ä	far	oi	oil	ᵺ	then	
e	let	ou	out	zh	measure	
ē	equal	u	cup			a in about
ėr	term	ù	put			e in taken
i	it	ü	rule	ə =		i in pencil
ī	ice	ch	child			o in lemon
o	hot	ng	long			u in circus

throt·tle (throt′l) a stick that controls the flow of steam or gas into an engine

tone (tōn) a voice sound of certain pitch showing feeling (When he spoke, I knew he was angry from his *tone* of voice.)

tour (tὺr) a trip that most often ends where it started (We took a *tour* of the new space center.)

tri·an·gle (trī′ang′gəl) a shape or object having three sides and three corners (Cut the square so that you get two *triangles.*)

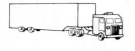

van

volcano

Uu

unique (yü nēk′) being the only one of its kind; very different (That old car is *unique.*)

uni·ver·si·ty (yü′nə vėr′sə tē) a place of higher learning

Vv

van (van) a truck for moving goods (When we moved, my mother hired a *van.*)●

vol·ca·no (vol kā′nō) **vol·ca·noes** *or* **vol·ca·nos** a mountain having an opening through which steam and lava pour●

Ww

waltz (wôlts) to dance a waltz—a smooth, flowing dance done in three-step timing (I *waltzed* with my father.)

wan·der (won′dər) to move about without any special direction

weath·er (weꟳH′ər) what it's like outside (We have been having rainy *weather* for two weeks.)

wed (wed) **wed·ded** *or* **wed; wed·ding** to marry

whin·ny (hwin′ē) **whin·nied; whin·ny·ing** to make a sound like a horse

whir (hwėr) **whirred; whir·ring** to move or turn quickly with a buzzing sound

win·dow·sill (win′dō sil′) a piece of wood or stone across the bottom of a window

wipe (wīp) **wiped; wip·ing** to clean or dry by rubbing ●

worth (wėrth) **1** the value of something (How much is your new ring *worth*?) **2** important enough for (Sometimes it's *worth* getting up early.)

wres·tle (res′əl) **wres·tled; wres·tling** to seize someone and try to trip or throw that person down (He *wrestled* me to the sidewalk.)

yawn (yôn) to open the mouth wide and breathe in when tired or bored

zoo (zü) a gathering of live animals for people to see ●

wipe

zoo

a	hat	ō	open	sh	she
ā	age	ô	order	th	thin
ä	far	oi	oil	ᴛʜ	then
e	let	ou	out	zh	measure
ē	equal	u	cup		a in about
ėr	term	u̇	put		e in taken
i	it	ü	rule	ə =	i in pencil
ī	ice	ch	child		o in lemon
o	hot	ng	long		u in circus

New Words

The following words are introduced in *Catching Glimpses*. Each is listed beside the number of the page on which it appears for the first time. The words printed in black are developmental words, and those printed in blue are new words that pupils can decode independently.

With the exception of derivatives (*gladness*, for example) only base forms are given.

Selection 2
15. Fletcher
Gwen
Jill
Rusty McGraw
unless
16. lineup
Marshall
17. braces
Erica
18. teammate
19. somebody
20. downhill
hopeless
22. grandstand

Selection 3
25. Archie
caller
Ethel
guinea pig
Kermit
menagerie
overflow
President
Quentin
Roosevelt
Theodore
toad

26. allow
27. Algonquin
favorite
lower
sneak
28. ill
mutt
obvious
retriever
sailboat
seriously
30. gallop
previous
though
31. backwards
indoors
lap
scramble
serious
slippery
throughout
32. curtain
Emily Spinach
horned toad

Selection 4
34. background
treasure

35. cardboard
include
rather
36. solid

Selection 5
38. canoe
explorer
French
Jacques
Joliet
Louis
Marquette
Mississippi
paddle
terribly
unknown
39. America
France
Frenchmen
govern
government
Messipi
Pacific
priest
40. journey
mostly
weather

41. reload
sandbar
struggle
swamp
swiftly
Wisconsin
42. buffalo
pipe
plentiful
streak
swift
43. Illinois
inland
44. countryside
discover
discovery
onward
seek
settle
45. Gulf
Mexico
settler
Spain
themselves
46. risk
wildlife
47. Canadian

351